# The Pastor as Counselor

# PASTORAL MINISTRY SERIES

(A series for pastors and laypeople, which addresses the nature and scope of ministry as a task of the congregation)

# The Pastor
# as Counselor

EDITED BY

Earl E. Shelp
and
Ronald H. Sunderland

The Pilgrim Press
NEW YORK

### Library of Congress Cataloging-in-Publication Data

The Pastor as counselor / edited by Earl E. Shelp and Ronald H. Sunderland.
    p.  cm.—(Pastoral ministry series)
    "Originally presented during the spring of 1989 as the Parker Memorial Lectures in Theology and Ministry at the Institute of Religion in Houston, Texas"—Acknowledgments.
    Includes bibliographical references.
    Contents: Counseling in ministry / James C. Fenhagen — Sermons as instruments of care and counseling / Samuel Southard—The moral context of counseling / James B. Nelson—Giving care through counseling / Liston O. Mills—Intimacy and relationships in counseling / Sidney Callahan—Healing in a theological perspective / Jasper N. Keith, Jr.
    ISBN 0-8298-0867-1 (pbk.) : $9.95
    1. Pastoral counseling. I. Shelp, Earl E., 1947–
II. Sunderland, Ronald H., 1929–. III. Title: Parker memorial lectures in theology and ministry. IV. Series.
BV4012.2.P255   1991
253.5—dc20
                                              90-49534
                                            CIP

Scripture quotations, unless otherwise indicated, are from the New Revised Standard Version Bible, copyright 1989, Division of Christian Education of the National Council of the Churches of Christ in the United States of America, and are used by permission.

The Pilgrim Press, 475 Riverside Drive, New York, NY 10115

Printed in the United States

# Contents

# Acknowledgments

THE ESSAYS IN THIS VOLUME WERE ORIGINALLY PRESENTED during the spring of 1989 as the Parker Memorial Lectures in Theology and Ministry at the Institute of Religion in Houston, Texas. The lectures perpetuate the memory of the late R. A. Parker, who served as trustee of the institute from 1964 to 1985. His genial and magnanimous spirit continues to inspire friends of the institute, whose support of the annual series is gratefully acknowledged. The contributors did double duty, making outstanding oral presentations and producing manuscripts in a timely manner. Our thanks are expressed to Ed DuBose, who assisted in the preparation of the final draft of the manuscripts. In addition to the individuals already named, the editors express their gratitude to Marion Meyer and Barbara Withers for their labors in behalf of the Pastoral Ministry series.

# Introduction

## Ronald H. Sunderland and Earl E. Shelp

PASTORAL CARE IN GENERAL AND PASTORAL COUNSELING as a particular form of pastoral care are elements of the praxis of ministry, the roots of which can be traced to the first-century church. While it is difficult to capture a detailed picture of the forms first-century congregations assumed, there is ample evidence that what we call pastoral ministry was an essential component in their respective identities. Victor Paul Furnish, for example, in depicting the scope of Paul's ministry, illustrates how strongly the apostle believed that the truth of the gospel (Gal. 2:14) "must manifest itself concretely in the life of the Christian community and in the individual lives of Christian believers wherever they are in the world."[1] Furnish declares that the Pauline correspondence is the product of Paul's pastoral activities, which loomed large in his apostolic work. Based on Paul's image of the church as Christ's body, and on Paul's own ministry, Furnish identifies pastoral care as "the work of monitoring, maintaining, and strengthening the vital functions by which the community of faith is quickened and built up into the

**Ronald H. Sunderland,** Ed.D., is associate director and senior research fellow in theology and ministry at the Foundation for Interfaith Research and Ministry, Houston, Texas.

**Earl E. Shelp,** Ph.D., is executive director and senior research fellow in theological ethics at the Foundation for Interfaith Research and Ministry, Houston, Texas.

body of Christ, as those vital functions are represented in its *koinonia*, its *eucharistia*, and its *diakonia*."[2]

According to D. Moody Smith, Paul's images of pastoral ministry in the early church are reinforced in the Johannine literature, where ministry is described as self-giving service conceived, in the first instance, as "intramural relationship." As Jesus lays down his life for his friends, so they must be willing to lay down their lives for one another. Smith proposes that the foot-washing pericope (John 13:1–17) is a symbol of "that practical ministry which defines the very life of the Johannine community. The community lives in and for such mutual service and apart from it, there is, effectually, no revelation, no faith, and particularly, no ministry and no church (see 1 John 4:7–8, 12, 20)."[3]

## Twentieth-Century Trends

By the 1950s, pastoral ministry emerged as an intellectual and practical discipline requiring specialized training, a trend leading ultimately to its separation from the general ministry of the congregation as a function peculiar to the clergy. In part, this trend may be explained by the tendency of congregants to perceive the role of the clergy as "specialists" hired to do the congregation's work. Members felt they were therefore excused from many congregational tasks, and, especially with respect to worship rituals, lay people more and more filled the role of spectators. Also, as it became clear that the church's practice of pastoral care (and of pastoral counseling in particular) must indeed be informed by the emerging social sciences, the widely held conviction that pastoral functions should be restricted to those who had received specialized training seemed vindicated.

There was a positive benefit to these trends. The church's pastoral ministry was deepened and strengthened by its reliance on insights gained from the secular sciences of psychology and psychotherapy. But there were accompanying losses. The theological and biblical nature of pastoral ministry and the role of congregants as active participants in congregational pastoral care were diminished.

The period beginning in the 1970s has been marked by two trends that are again changing the shape of pastoral care. First, there is a slow but steady resurgence in the recovery of pastoral care as a ministry of the congregation, calling on the services of both ordained and lay ministers.[4] Second, there is a growing emphasis on the embedding of the ministry of pastoral counseling within the biblical and theological tradition and within the congregation.[5]

It is to the second of these concerns that the essays of this volume are addressed. Pastoral counseling, as a specialized ministry within the church's general pastoral ministry, is assumed to be restricted to those members, usually clergy, who have received training in this discipline and who practice their respective levels of pastoral counseling under appropriate oversight or supervision. While few pastors have completed formal training in pastoral counseling, clergy are faced with expectations of congregants and of the general public that they are competent to undertake personal and family counseling. But, in light of the multitude of other expectations placed on clergy, it is also true that few clergy can and do undertake more than minimal responsibilities in the area of pastoral counseling. Most parish pastors may assume a small counseling case load, referring to qualified therapists (pastoral and secular) situations requiring extended or intensive counseling. It is well for pastors to be fully aware of their limitations and to acknowledge the need for oversight of their counseling activities for reasons identified below, as well as to continue their education in counseling skills.

Regardless of the level of training, however, virtually all clergy can expect to be asked for counseling help in the ordinary course of their duties. The following essays are written not to instruct pastors in *how* to counsel but to assist them to understand and draw upon those biblical and theological precepts and sources that are particularly helpful in identifying pastoral counseling within the general ministry of the congregation. They indicate what makes counseling *pastoral* counseling.

## The Essays

James Fenhagen sets the pastoral counseling function first within the biblical concepts of wisdom literature. The pastor in a local congregation serves as the bearer of wise counsel. Second, this ministry is set in a vision of human life that is deeply concerned with moral integrity and personal righteousness rooted in the holiness of God. Third, wisdom literature emphasizes an unfailing concern with practical, day-to-day living. Fenhagen examines the vocation of the counselor against this backdrop, calling on pastors to draw on the wisdom they have gathered from their own life experiences and self-awareness. He urges that pastoral counseling, as a ministry, be based on the premise that, by the power of the Holy Spirit, it is possible to help others find a direction for their lives that is consistent with what they are created to be. For parish ministers, the location of this ministry is the congregation, which can become a community of wellness when ministries of spiritual companionship and direction support that of pastoral counseling.

Samuel Southard examines the extent to which preaching ministries may be an extension of pastors' counseling roles. Like Fenhagen, he finds a strong link between pastoral counseling and wisdom literature, which, he proposes, asks two questions about preaching: What is the capacity of hearers to receive the truth about themselves and God at this time in their lives? And how is the preacher's presentation of the truth about God and self conditioned by his or her own character and need for security and recognition?

Southard identifies four resources in wisdom literature: universal, or "international," intelligence; moral guidance; prophetic insight; and the incarnation of wisdom in Christ. International intelligence, so called because the sayings to which the term applies are recognized as wise in a variety of cultures, may mean that both preacher and congregation perceive the world and themselves through the same wisdom; their common assumptions reduce anxiety because they speak the same language. Where this commonality does not occur, the possibility of fundamental misperceptions of meaning between preacher and congregants due to lack of common ground may inhibit the development of pastoral relationships by means of the sermon. Southard illustrates such a breakdown with incidents related to the membership of divorced and single members in congregations in which pastors' stereotypes of families are based on a two-parent, two-child home, and the sexual stereotypes of many male preachers, which may offend and alienate congregants and thereby close rather than open channels of communication and caring.

Southard approaches his second resource, moral guidance, through the lens of the deceit and secrecy he observed in young, former drug users, and the ministry of preaching in which he was engaged at the time. He found that his attempt to address their personal and theological needs through open sharing and discussion risked alienating other congregants.

The third resource, prophetic insight, inspires prophetic preaching, the pastoral function of which is to expose the defensive detachment of people from the way that God has created them to be with God and one another. Such preaching brings with it self-insight and the potential for change.

The fourth resource is Christ, the wisdom of God. Preaching Christ, the wisdom of God, in a congregation of obsessed, co-dependent people identifies for them Paul's analysis of deception as a basic decision between life and death. Pastoral preaching reflects Paul's identification of substitutes for spiritual life and the contrasting offer of the living and growing alternative in Christ. Southard concludes that, as pastors seek to extend the congregation's pastoral ministry through preaching, they would likely reach members and serve their needs through a combination of power they did not control and wisdom that remained beyond their understanding.

Whereas Fenhagen and Southard look for biblical insights derived from wisdom literature to suggest the *form* of pastoral counseling, proposing that the pastor's task is to assist people to develop a sense of self-awareness and self-determination in the context of the biblical message, James Nelson views the counseling function, and therefore the identity of the counselor, from his perspective as an ethical contextualist. He is concerned with direction and content, particularly as the latter is related to counselors' perceptions of themselves as sexual beings. He finds four overlapping, interconnected moral contexts that are inescapable in counseling: the fundamental moral purpose of counseling; the theological ethical commitments in the counseling method itself; the counselor's basic attitudes and actions regarding respect and coercion; and the moral community within which counseling is offered.

Nelson examines the moral and theological issues that revolve around people's awareness of their physical bodies: the times when individuals have felt at one with their bodies have been "too few, too fragmentary." He asks how this self-body alienation occurred, sketching the various attempts made to address spirit-body dualism. He concludes that moral understanding is significantly bodily, reminding readers that both Judaism and Christianity are at once rich and ambiguous in body attitudes. He addresses awareness of human sexuality from the perspectives of moral understanding, caring, and "connecting." Human alienation from bodily feelings (particularly on the part of males) takes a terrible toll, since our capacities for compassion and connecting, like our capacity for moral understanding, are bodily. This is illustrated in reference to male-female attitudes to sexual stereotypes, sexism, and homosexuality. Sexual stereotypes remind us that we are all "body people," a fact we have learned in the context of bodily fears, envies, shame, and guilt.

These images are incarnated in a pastoral encounter depicting one family's response to two gay friends living with HIV disease. The story highlights graphically our capacity to sense that we are the embodiment of healing, power, and connecting with others. When that happens, it is a moment for thanks.

The common bond that links all three essays is the writers' sense that pastoral counseling is threaded through and through with moral guidance: counselors after all shape their counseling and the relationships that evolve from it in the context of their respective faith stances. Liston Mills, also, uses this as his starting point. He identifies the discipline of pastoral counseling as an expression of care and proceeds to examine how the term "pastoral" qualifies "care" and, subsequently, "counseling." Pastoral counseling is located within the *cure-of-souls* tradition. In its narrowest sense, it refers to the more intensive dimension of the larger tasks of ministry, that is, to conversations regarding interpersonal, moral, or spiritual guidance. Care reflects a theological diagnosis of human distress that serves to define its general meaning as well as that of its specific expression in counseling.

The emphasis evident by the mid 1950s of the relevance of dynamic personality theory for pastoral work led to intense study of this arena, at the cost of neglecting, even abandoning, the theological roots of pastoral care, and further, of separating care and counseling. Care was rooted more fully in the communal life, meanings, and traditions of the church, whereas counseling became less clear as to its theological character and intent. Yet pastoral counseling as care became an invitation to relationship and to a community that understands itself to depend upon the gift of life in grace. Pastoral counseling as care invites us to participate in a relationship in which it is safe to be both autonomous and dependent, to discover what we believe, to accept judgment, and to admit our need for a wisdom greater than our own. Pastoral counseling thus offers blessing and fosters hope.

Sidney Callahan examines counseling from the perspective of the intimacy that is intrinsic to that relationship, but the reader quickly senses she is addressing concerns similar to those of the preceding essays: the moral commitment of the counselor and the ethical content implicit or explicit in the counselor's activities and words.

Callahan proposes that the intimacy that is basic to counseling differs uniquely from that which characterizes other types of relationships in that it is time-structured, short-term, unilateral, and confidentially privileged. It produces a particular set of moral and ethical questions. She points to Stephen Toulmin's distinction between an ethics of intimacy and an ethics of strangers: in an ethics of strangers one resorts to universal principles and applies them impartially, whereas those who coexist in intimate relationships can make specific, case-by-case decisions arising out of their shared values, experience, and special knowledge of particular events. An ethics of intimacy grows out of, but extends beyond, an ethics of strangers, with respect to counseling relationships.

As in all intimate relationships, the counselor can impede or harm others through ignorance, carelessness, weakness, or moral flaws. It is incumbent upon the counselor, therefore, to be open constantly to self-examination and self-criticism, to have a strong moral commitment, and to desire to be well and to serve competently. Continuing education and supervision are essential to this enterprise. Callahan asserts that most of the ethical problems in intimate counseling involve the use of power that counselors possess by virtue of their roles. It is a further abuse of the counseling relationship to exploit it through the imposition of the counselor's religious or moral system at a time when the other person is distraught and needy. Finally, counselors must apply an ethics of intimacy to themselves and their own spiritual well-being.

Jasper Keith pursues many of the same motifs, but he does

so from an experiential model rather than the more didactic and theoretical models of the other essays. Yet this essay, also, assumes a particular theological context within which counselors function, and his ethic is one that places the highest emphasis on the value and integrity of the individual in counseling.

He builds his chapter around the story of John Smith, who arrives at his doctor's office with chest pains. The case serves as a basis for addressing such issues as the relationship between "health" and the presence or absence of "sickness" or disability, the general expectations of most people that physicians as technicians can and should fix whatever it is that is functioning inefficiently, and whether Smith's "feeling well" means that he has been "healed."

When Smith's progress appears to be at a standstill, he is referred by his physician to a pastoral counselor. The counselor begins not with "what" questions, which treat Smith as an object to be probed, but with "who" questions, which address him personally and invite him to disclose himself and enter into a relationship.

Keith then examines the way a pastoral counselor facilitates a healing process with Smith, identifying empathic listening, asking the right questions in a timely manner, engaging in the depth work of counseling through shared language and symbols, and following through the tedious work of the counseling process. The unique aspect of *pastoral* counseling revolves around discerning and addressing the faith questions in Smith's story.

Keith closes with a discourse on theological reflection on the counseling process, beginning with the Old Testament concept of *shalom*, meaning "wholeness," "completeness," "soundness," and "well-being." The issue that determines the Old Testament perception of health is human relatedness to God. Fulfilment, wholeness, salvation, however, remain partial and incomplete. John Smith remains far from "wholeness," but his new-found "health" is far more than he had ever known. Smith's counselor, like Smith, is also far from whole, complete, mature, perfect. Salvation, then, may be relatively fulfilled, but it remains as a promise and belongs to God's future. Counseling, from this perspective, is an analog of the journey toward salvation. Each party in the relationship struggles with partial fulfilment, but each does so in the company of the other.

## Appropriate Supervision

Finally, a word must be added regarding the submission of clergy counseling to some appropriate level of supervision. The scope of the essays ranges from broad levels of pastoral care, such as "wise counsel" and spiritual direction, to more formalized or professional counseling. Even in the broad levels a strong argument can be made for at least informal peer review of counseling for reasons similar to those justifying such review among physicians and other professionals. The essays direct pastors to recognize both their own vulnerability and that of people they counsel. For example, Mills suggests that neophytes in counseling are apt to believe they should always know and understand what is happening in their interchanges with people, an assumption he suggests is ill-founded. Tragedy is prone to occur when counselors also believe they know fully what it is that recipients of counsel need to know or do in order to extricate themselves from their problems. Pastors must therefore heed one of the critical lessons learned from the secular fields of clinical psychology and psychotherapy, namely, that it is mandatory that counselors' functions must be subject to the scrutiny of professional peers in order to safeguard both the integrity of the counseling relationship and that of the counselor and the person I counsel within that relationship.

Three ends are served when counseling is undertaken under supervision. First, the person being counseled has some reassurance of the integrity and competence of the counselor and the counseling process. Second, the counselor is held accountable for that integrity and competence, a necessary element for the protection of both parties. Third, the counselor is able to use the process as a basis for continuing education. Indeed, it is not too strong a statement to make that pastors act irresponsibly when they engage in unsupervised counseling. The intricate web of relationships based on the intimacy of sharing and complex intrapersonal and interpersonal dynamics in the lives of both counselors and persons being counseled makes it necessary for the protection of both that counseling be open to supervision.

These essays provide an intriguing challenge to pastors to examine their pastoral counseling functions within the context of the universal charge laid upon the congregation to be a place where pastoral care is concretized in a ministry of compassion informed by the biblical and theological roots and traditions of God's people. Pastors have much to gain from reflection on their own life experiences, and the depth of their spiritual formation will shape how those experiences are used in counseling relationships. Nevertheless, clergy who engage in pastoral counseling must also be informed by the insights into interpersonal and intrapersonal functions available in the social sciences.

The authors call on clergy to integrate insights gained from the secular disciplines with their spiritual, ethical, and theological systems. Biblical and theological meanings and symbols will assist pastors to offer a counseling ministry that grows out of the highest ethical and moral precepts and that serves the needs of those being counseled.[6] Such a ministry is aimed at assisting individuals and families to reach toward fulfilment, in the biblical sense of that term. Only when these conditions are fulfilled is it appropriate to affix the term "pastoral" to "care" and "counseling."

## CHAPTER 1

# Counseling in Ministry
## Reflections on the Pastor as Counselor in a Congregational Setting

## James C. Fenhagen

Not long ago I was engaged in conversation with a group of ordained men and women about their sense of identity as pastors within the local congregation. One of them said to me, "Whenever I think of my role as a counselor to people in need, I tend to think of myself as second best. There are others out there who are better trained and more knowledgeable than I am, and when I think about it, I feel a bit depressed."

Pastoral counseling, in whatever form it takes, is integral to the ministry of the Christian church. We get in trouble, however, when we confuse this ministry with the therapeutic disciplines to which it is obviously related. I propose that the roots of the pastoral ministry are not in the psychological disciplines but in the scriptural witness to the gift of wisdom in human growth, a witness that affirms the importance of all

**The Rev. James C. Fenhagen,** D.D., is dean and president of General Theological Seminary, New York.

the activity that takes place in the congregation that affirms one person's call to care for another.

I will develop this thesis in three sections: (1) a brief examination of the biblical roots of the pastoral task, (2) the vocational implications that derive from these roots, and (3) counseling as ministry within the congregational setting.

## Counseling and the Gift of Wisdom

When we think of the scriptural roots of pastoral care, many familiar images come immediately to mind. When Jesus offered forgiveness to the woman taken in adultery, he was offering pastoral care. His words to her, "Go . . . and . . . do not sin again [John 8:11]," offered in the context of a relationship that embodied both compassion and respect, provided direction for the woman's life. When Jesus asked Bartimaeus, the blind beggar, what he would have him do, Jesus was throwing Bartimaeus back on his own inner resources. He was inviting Bartimaeus to move from a life of willed dependence to a place where he could draw on his own inner wisdom and strength (Mark 10:51). The ministry of counseling, I suggest, has its roots in the gift of wisdom that God offers to us all. As the writer of Proverbs explains, it is the intent of his collection of sayings that we may know wisdom and instruction, understand words of insight, and receive instruction in "wise dealing, righteousness, justice, and equity [Prov. 1:2–3]."

Like all the great collections in the Bible, wisdom literature has many themes,[1] some of which have a more contemporary ring than others. The conviction that God rewards the righteous and punishes the wicked comes under more and more scrutiny as the wisdom writers wrestle with the realities that life presents. It is this profound wrestling breaking out in unexpected places that constitutes what some scholars have referred to as the existential theme that so deeply influenced the wisdom of Jesus. This theme, which is echoed in such passages as the familiar "For everything there is a season, and a time for every matter under heaven," from Ecclesiastes or in the anguished questioning of God's justice that we hear from Job, reflects a deep concern for the meaning of life and for our capacity to cope. But what makes this literature unique is the conviction that however life is lived, its quality and fruitfulness are directly related to the moral vision that shapes it. Wisdom, then, in the existential tradition of scripture, is concerned with questions of meaning and purpose, with moral integrity, and with the way we respond to the problems of life on a day-to-day basis—all in the context of a belief that the meaning of life is reflected in the nature of creation itself, if only we have eyes to see.

## Wisdom as the Art of Living

A cartoon in the *New Yorker* magazine depicted two owls sitting on a tree. The first owl, with a rather distasteful look on its face, says to the other, "You're wise, but you lack tree-smarts."[2] The wisdom of scripture by contrast might be described as "tree-smarts with depth." The wisdom of which the Bible speaks is insight, sharpened by struggle and infused with grace. "Wisdom," in the biblical sense of the word, writes Diane Bergund,

> is within the world but beyond human grasp. It is like the meaning implanted by God in creation—the divine mystery of creation itself. The mystery always calls us out, always beckons to women and men, cajoling, enticing, challenging them to search out the secrets of creation and life. And yet, as the wisdom poem in Job so accurately states, only God understands the way to it, only God "knows the place."[3]

In a Pendle Hill pamphlet entitled "The Art of the Every Day," Zoe White tells of her ministry to a fifty-five-year-old woman dying of cancer in the prime of her life.

> On the morning of Francis' death, as I stood by her bedside, I made a secret resolve somewhere deep in my being which has only recently come to the surface. I made an agreement with God that from that day onward, everything I have to say about God, everything I have to say theologically, has to be able to stand with me by Francis' beside. If it cannot stand at the side of death, if it cannot stand by the side of a fifty-five-year-old woman who wanted to live to see the trees again, it better not stand at all because it is probably not worth very much.[4]

It is this understanding of God's wisdom that is echoed by the Psalmist in words we know so well, "Out of the depths I cry to you, O LORD. Lord, hear my voice! Let your ears be attentive to the voice of my supplications [Ps. 130:1–2]." It is this wisdom that pastoral counseling needs both to look at and to impart.

## *Counseling, Psychotherapy, and Spiritual Direction*

In an unpublished address, Gerald May made distinctions between pastoral counseling, psychotherapy, and spiritual direction that I have found particularly helpful. Despite obvious overlaps, he suggests that psychotherapy is interested primarily in self-understanding, pastoral counseling in self-determination, and spiritual direction in self-surrender to the discerned will of God. All pastors offer help in areas that border on psychotherapy. All pastors, it is to be hoped, offer help in spiritual direction. There are also pastors who are specifically trained in the disciplines of pastoral psychotherapy and spiritual direction who are very much needed as resources for the local church. The pastor serving in a congregation is concerned primarily with the task of assisting people in greater self-determination in the context of a particular vision about what life is about.

I have found the wisdom literature helpful in establishing this vision, although I acknowledge that some of the didactic elements are too culturally limited to be of much help today. What is of help is the understanding that the pastor in a local congregation serves as a bearer of wise counsel, rooted in scripture and informed by the psychological and sociological insights present in any contemporary understanding of human growth. To serve as bearers of this wisdom, we pastors must root ourselves not in the field of psychotherapy but in an approach to life reflected in our biblical heritage. Certain themes that emerge from wisdom literature seem particularly helpful.

First, the wisdom of the scriptures not only holds to a view of life that is unfailingly real, it points to an understanding of human growth that places emphasis on the capacity of a person to stand on his or her own. Even in his most wretched state, Job was never totally helpless and unworthy of respect. This means that the pastoral task is focused not so much on those who are broken and needy as on building structures that contribute to "wellness" by encouraging the people to whom we minister to draw on the wisdom that is God-given and within them. The search for wisdom is deeply connected with the capacity for memory, the cultivation of which, as I will point out later, is central to the pastoral task.

Second, the wisdom of the scriptures presents us with a vision of human life that is deeply concerned for moral integrity and personal righteousness rooted in the holiness of God. "The fear of the Lord is the beginning of wisdom," writes the author of Proverbs, "and the knowledge of the Holy One is insight [Prov. 9:10–11]." When we trace this theme of moral integrity into the New Testament, the vision is considerably enlarged. What we are talking about is a view of life infused by the vision of the kingdom of God where human compassion and the concern for justice and mercy take precedence over a personal morality that narrows our boundaries and feeds on itself. Pastoral care, therefore, has a profoundly moral dimension, and it is engaging men and women around the great moral themes that echo from the scriptures that makes the ministry of the pastor unique. When this emphasis is lacking in our ministry, a spiritual vacuum is left that no other profession can adequately fill.

And finally, we see in the wisdom literature an unfailing concern with the practical, day-by-day living out of life that is vocational rather than happenstance. Life is a gift that is reflected in God's plan for creation. Humankind is not here by accident. This means that the task of living involves making those everyday decisions that make use of our gifts and allow us to discern where God is leading us. Such discernment can involve something as basic as the way we use time or as profound as the way we prepare for death. The pastoral ministry of the church is always concerned with the sick and the dying and with those who have been crushed by life and need respite and support. Pastors offer this support, however, not as lone individuals but as part of a community that reflects in its life the ministry of Jesus to others. A counselor in the wisdom tradition is an artist of the spirit helping people find the brushes and the paints they need to create, through the limitless grace of God, their own lives.

## The Vocation of the Counselor

The vocation of the counselor in the life of the church is to be a wisdom bearer in the name of Christ. As counselors we can speak of wisdom to others when we are in touch with the wisdom that is in ourselves. We can help others embrace the vision of the kingdom that Jesus presents to us when we have begun to come to terms with the moral integrity in our lives and find in Christ the freedom to be who we say we are. We can speak of direction and purpose when our own vocational identity is clear. With these three concerns in mind, let us look then at the vocation of the Christian counselor.

## Discovering the Wisdom in Ourselves

At the heart of the vocation of the wisdom bearer lies a courageous willingness to face the inconsistencies of one's own life and the world in which we live. Life does not always work out. God does not always answer prayers the way we want them answered. Good people have terrible things happen to them, and we ourselves do things that are totally inconsistent with who we say we are. It is in owning these inconsistencies, and the truth that lies behind them, that wisdom is deepened.

In a moving short story entitled "The Promise of Rain," Peter Taylor writes about a father's reflection on a long-awaited encounter he has just had with his oldest son. Father and son had been estranged for many years, and on the son's initiative they meet to talk about the breakdown that had occurred between them. The meeting is brief, but a connection is made—a healing connection that causes the father to muse as the son walks out the door. "I was fifty," the father says, "but I had just discovered what it means to see the world through another man's eyes. It is a discovery you are lucky to make at any age, and one that is no less marvelous whether you make it at fifty or fifteen. It is only then that the world, as you have seen it through your own eyes, will begin to tell you things about yourself."[5]

It is this capacity for continuous learning about oneself that is one clear mark of the counseling vocation. As counselors we cannot identify with another's struggle unless we are in touch with the struggle in our own lives. The burden the counselor bears is the constant threat of isolation from oneself that occurs when we become the role we play. As we all know so well, when living out the role of the counselor becomes a substitute for authentic human interaction, our capacity to provide genuine help is severely limited. I cannot identify with the pain of another unless I am in touch with the pain in myself—but in touch in such a way that I am able to listen without projecting my pain on the person who comes for help. The discipline of effective counseling demands that we not burden others with the wounds of our own vulnerability, but we cannot avoid doing this unless we know where these wounds are lodged and are able to incorporate them in our sense of self.

In the book of Proverbs there is a saying that beautifully sums up what self-awareness is about: "Can fire be carried in the bosom without burning one's clothes? Or can one walk on hot coals without scorching the feet? [Prov. 6:27–28]." It is in the acknowledgment of the burning and the scorching that wisdom is forged, for wisdom is insight, formed in struggle and infused by grace. The gift of counsel comes when the wisdom that has been formed in us by the Spirit encounters the deep truth that comes from listening to another. The gift of counsel is what makes pastoral counseling an act of ministry.

## Moral Integrity and Personal Righteousness

Moral integrity is a second critical element in the vocation of a counselor whose self-identity is shaped by the gospel tradition. It goes hand in hand with a thirst for personal righteousness. Moral integrity involves acting in ways that are consistent with who we are. The thirst for personal righteousness has to do with our desire and our will to fill the gaps between what we say and what we do. In the Christian tradition the vision that empowers us is the person of Jesus.

The gap between what we say and what we do is the focal point of all moral integrity. The tragedy that occurs when a pastor takes sexual advantage of a person who comes for help is that it destroys both trust and the vision of what life in Christ is intended to be. Unfortunately, the problem of seduction by those in the helping professions is widespread, especially among the clergy. Recently I saw a young woman who had just ended a long affair with a married pastor to whom she had gone for help. The scars left by this encounter were deep: disillusionment with the church, loss of trust in the clergy, but more especially the crippling effects of a deep sense of shame caused by the fear that, since the pastor was the holy person, she was solely at fault. The pastor involved is no longer in the ordained ministry. His wife and children have left him, and this very gifted man is attempting to rebuild his life. In reflecting on what happened he acknowledged the deepening gap between what in public he stood for and what in private he actually did. What he lacked was a thirst for righteousness that was strong enough to overcome a deep need that was out of control.

Moral integrity has to do at a very deep level with saying yes and no. When we utter in any language the words yes or no, we are speaking two of the most important words that exist in the human vocabulary. The care with which we choose these words determines not only the quality of relationships with other people but the moral integrity of our relationship to God. We all too often say yes to people for all the wrong reasons, or else we fail to say a clear no when we very much need to. The hardest no, of course, is the one we say to ourselves. If we are serious about our faith, we know that there are hard choices to be made if the way we live is to reflect what we believe. There is no way we can reflect the values implicit in Jesus's vision of the kingdom without its affecting the way we live: our moral values, the pace of our lives, the way we spend money, the way we trust people, or indeed, the way we treat ourselves. As Jesus makes so clear, the greatest enemy of faith is not what is external to us but our capacity for self-deception. We too often say yes with our lips without coming to terms with the no that we express by the way we live.

All of us, I suspect, find ourselves coaxed into doing things for or giving to organizations about which we have little interest. For a number of years I served on the board of an organization but never attended a meeting. When the director of the organization would call to ask me to continue, I explained that I could not attend the meetings and thought it best to resign. Each year he managed to persuade me that for some reason having my name on the list of board members was helpful to him, and so I would give a reluctant yes. I found, however, that the no that I was really saying was poisoning my relationship with this man whom I had once respected. I began to avoid seeing him and found myself unconsciously resisting returning his calls. A year ago I invited this man out to lunch and resigned from the board. I gave him a clear no without apology, explaining why I could not serve. As a result a new kind of relationship has developed between us. My clear no has made it possible for a new kind of yes to emerge—a yes that now has the integrity that for so long was missing.

## Purpose and Identity

Pastoral counseling is a ministry of the church. It is based on the premise that by the power of the Holy Spirit working through people, it is possible to help others find directions for their lives that are consistent with what they were created to be. To do this, the counselor's identity in Christ must itself be secure. This is the third element in the formation of the vocation of the pastoral counselor that I believe to be critical to the way our ministries are expressed. Problems of role confusion, or the inability to deal consistently with transference and projection, occur when our own centers are weak. Carl Jung once wrote that the care of the individual is the center of life. If a person allows his or her center to be dulled by the crowd, dissipated by business or pleasure, or go unchallenged, that person has committed the supreme treason. It is treasonable because it is a betrayal of ourselves.

I have a friend whose daughter had been badly disfigured as a child. After many operations and much love by gifted and caring people, Susan emerged as a beautiful young woman whose scars were a mark of her beauty. For several years she worked in France, moving from one job to another as she struggled to master the language. On a particular day as she was riding home on the Paris subway, she looked up and saw sitting across from her a mother with a badly disfigured daughter. Susan found herself drawn to that child as if by a magnet. When mother and daughter got off the subway, Susan followed and finally caught up, and poured out to the mother and daughter the story of her own healing. The encounter ended with an embrace and many tears, but as Susan told her father later, it was a meeting in which Christ was profoundly present. "When I saw that child," Susan said, "I knew I had to make contact. It had to do in some mysterious way with what my life was about."

There are two great words in the Christian vocabulary that are central to our understanding of the Christian life. The first word is *vocation* and the second is *ministry*. These are, of course, related to each other and deeply embedded in the sacrament of Holy Baptism. "Vocation" expresses our identity as Christians; "ministry" describes the many ways in which we live this vocation out. "Vocation" describes our sense of being, "ministry" our sense of doing. Identity is the answer to the questions, Who am I? and What is my life for? Our identities as persons are formed over a long period of time in response to the many influences that shape our lives. Our identities as Christians are gifts, reinforcing who we are as healthy human beings but enlarging who we are and what our lives are about. To claim the identity that gives me my vocation is to acknowledge the presence and spirit of Jesus Christ within me. I am, to put it rather simplistically, Jim plus Jesus, and I cannot understand myself fully apart from this relationship. To understand myself this way is to know in the core of my being that my life counts for something. I am here for a purpose, and it is in living out this purpose—this vocation—that I most express who I am. In knowing who I am in Christ, and by nurturing who I am in Christ, I am able to be present to another person from the center of my being, for it is Jesus Christ who makes the connection.

## Professionalism and Pastoral Care

The ministry of pastoral counseling is a vocational ministry that is central to the life of the church. If the church is a community of healing and care, it requires, in addition to those pastors who serve a local congregation, persons with special skills to respond to special situations—pastoral psychotherapists, hospital chaplains, counselors to those wrestling with chemical dependency—to name but a few; but even so, the roots of this ministry lie not in the field of psychology but in the wisdom of scripture. The biblical story provides the grounding and the vision that give birth to vocation. Psychology and the other social sciences provide us with the knowledge of human growth and behavior that, when learned well, enable us to live out our pastoral vocation in ways that take seriously the complexity of the human struggle and our own involvement in it. When the psychological disciplines are seen as the servants of vocation, and not the other way around, the role of the pastor has an integrity and importance that is unique. In the remainder of this essay, therefore, I turn my attention to the local congregation and explore what the counseling ministry contributes to its well-being, who does it, and what helps it take place. It is, as the scriptures remind us, by bearing one another's burdens that we "fulfill the law of Christ [Gal. 6:2]."

## Counseling as Ministry in the Congregational Setting

In his provocative book *Professionalism and Pastoral Care*, Alastair Campbell writes:

> The need to encourage a diversity of gifts within the Christian community requires great caution in allocating a dominant role to ordained ministers in the task of pastoral care. Rather than seeking a specialist counseling role, clergy should specialize in the pastoral aspects of their preaching and priestly functions and should use their positions of leadership in the congregation to encourage the caring ministry of all Christians. . . . When counseling expertise is acquired, it is not a status to be guarded, but a gift to be fully shared.[6]

My own training for the ordained ministry took place in the 1950s, when the pastoral psychology movement was at its height. As a counterbalance to the moralism and coercive manipulation, often based on sheer ignorance, that was all too prevalent in the pastoral ministries of clergy, the insights of Freud and Jung and the nondirective pastoral style of Carl Rogers and Seward Hiltner were made normative in theological education. My excitement about what I had learned moved me to do additional work in clinical pastoral education and to sharpen my understanding and skill as a pastoral counselor. Effectiveness in the pastoral ministry, as I had come to see it, was related to the number of people who came to my office for counseling. And so, the more available I became, the more people came for help—and a predictable few came more often than others, as they moved from one dependent relationship to another. It came as a shock then, indeed, a blow that hurt, when it was suggested by a member of my vestry whom I very much respected that if I would spend as much time with those whose lives were relatively together as I did with those whose lives were in crisis, the parish might really get going. By assuming the role of parish therapist I was creating a dependent community that was finding it increasingly difficult to take responsibility for anything, including even caring for themselves.

I have probably had no encounter in my thirty-five years of ministry more important than my encounter with that vestryman. He was for me a profound source of wisdom. There is clearly a place for pastoral psychotherapy as a supportive ministry in the life of the church, and we need clergy and laity who are both gifted and especially trained to do it. But psychotherapy is not the normal ministry of the parish priest. The ministry of counseling in the life of the congregation is a ministry of practical wisdom concerned with helping healthy people use their lives in ways that are productive and holy.

I suggest that there are three points of entry into the life of the congregation that might help strengthen the potential for genuine caring and deepening wholeness. They have to do with (1) creating an environment of wellness, (2) developing a communal moral vision, and (3) broadening ministries of care. In this final section I shall explore these areas briefly in the context of their implications for the ministries of ordained persons as well as the people of congregations themselves.

## Creating an Environment of Wellness

A wellness model of pastoral care places emphasis on building a system within the life of the congregation that affirms the strength that human beings possess and encourages them to take responsibility for their own lives while offering support to those around them. It is based on the recognition, recently made very visible by the popularity of Edwin Friedman's book *Generation to Generation*,[7] that a congregation is a complex network of often highly charged emotional connections. What happens in the family of one parishioner, or in the family of the pastor, both the immediate family and the family of origin, can affect the dynamics of a committee meeting or the clarity of a cry for help. What is required of the pastor is sufficient self-knowledge and awareness of what is going on to serve as a "nonanxious presence" to keep the connection from becoming blocked and communication open.

A community of wellness can be anchored around visible points of emphasis that make clear the nature of God's care for the wholeness of creation. Preaching, if it is in touch with the people it addresses, is always a ministry of pastoral care. The proclamation of the word is never in a vacuum, since through the work of the Spirit, a relationship is established where those who respond are able to take the word into themselves for their own empowerment. In the tradition from which I come, which has its counterpart in other traditions, the sacramental liturgies of healing and reconciliation and the eucharistic emphasis on hospitality and life in Christ all serve as signposts by which a sense of healing, hope, and care for others is reinforced. A liturgical service of healing not only links us visibly with the healing power of God but reminds us that in Christ we all possess healing gifts to be shared. When a priest pronounces the forgiveness of God to troubled penitents, it is a reminder to them that they also in Christ are called to be the bearers of forgiveness to others. Ordination is the church's act of making one person a representative symbol to remind others of what they are called to be and do.

The pastoral possibilities of congregational life are almost beyond imagining. Some have to do with simply paying attention to what goes on and keeping connections open. Others are highly visible and critically important to the way people understand themselves. Still others are as low key and ongoing as a telephone call to someone who is alone or a note of thanks for a job well done or the steady offering of prayer for the ministries that go on. In a very real way, prayer and care are synonymous. You cannot have one without the other.

## Developing a Moral Vision That Is Compassionate and Wise

Don Browning, the distinguished professor of religion and psychological studies at the Divinity School of the University of Chicago, argues in his book *Religious Ethics and Pastoral Care* for the reconnection of pastoral care with its moral and ethical roots. Echoing very loudly what I believe to be some of the major themes in the wisdom literature of scripture, he calls on congregations to reconstitute their caring practices "that they might become more adept in the skills of practical thinking." "Such critical practical thinking," he writes, "is inevitably moral thinking. . . . Under the pressures of pluralism the very goals of our care often come under question. To reconstitute these goals our care must once again be guided by a normative discipline—by a critical and practical religious ethos or moral theology."[8]

Most congregations I know of are not the "communities of moral discourse" that Browning argues for. Churches all too often become sounding boards for those who are inclined to make moral pronouncements on issues about which they have given little, if any, critical thought or who, in the name of acceptance, support issues of behavior and moral vision that are never examined. The gospel that the Christian church proclaims is a gospel of forgiveness, but forgiveness means little if there is no sense that our lives have fallen short of what we were created to be.

If we are to make sense of the wisdom dimension of pastoral care, we must also come to terms once again with the demand that law and the prophets make on human behavior. But, because the society in which we live is complex, the ethical norms that constitute our response to the commandments of God and the prophetic witness to these commandments are also complex. We can never be bearers of wisdom to others, much less ministers of compassion, until we have moved beneath the surface of those shrill voices that are so quick to judge who is right and who is wrong to a soul-searching exploration of how indeed the moral vision that the Gospels hold up for us is lived out in our own day. To do this the circle of disagreement must be widened and the temperature of debate lowered so that a new consensus, or at least an agreement to disagree, can be reached. There is no task of any more importance in the life of the church today. It is a task that must involve every age and every group to which we have access, for without a moral vision, ministries of counseling have no theological roots.

## Broadening Ministries of Care

When I first arrived as the new rector of a suburban congregation in South Carolina, where I served for five years, I was invited by a parishioner to join him at an open meeting of Alcoholics Anonymous. This, he said, was his ministry to me. Not long afterwards I had a call from a family in crisis over a problem involving alcohol abuse. I called my friend, who went with me to make the call. He was the counselor. I provided support.

In every congregation there are ministries of care that are already going on. What is needed is a way of legitimizing these ministries, strengthening them, and learning from them so that they are trusted by others. Men and women who have been through the experience of loss themselves can be given the help they need to be counselors to others who are grieving. And the list goes on. Parents who have struggled with the problems of adolescent offspring can be of immense help to others. In a congregation I served in Washington, D.C., there was a long-established telephone ministry aimed at providing support and counsel to elderly persons who lived alone. The experience these unsung counselors had gained over the years was of immense help in establishing telephone counselors in other areas.

There is a growing body of material dealing with what is

now the discipline of crisis intervention. Its aim is to provide better training for those called to intervene in the many crises that confront us on a day-to-day basis. Crisis counseling is short term. It can be carried on effectively at quite different levels of sophistication. Its purpose is to help people recover their capacity to cope when threatened by stress. When a crisis occurs in our lives—whether it be the result of loss or sickness or an unexpected event or a job change—our self-perception is threatened, stress increases, our options become unclear, and we loose our capacity to act. Where ministries are developed that understand these dynamics, immense healing and growth can take place. It is the task of a congregation concerned about this level of pastoral care within its own life and in the community it serves to provide the training and support that are needed to call these ministries forth and make them as effective as possible.

## Spiritual Support and Companionship

There is a fundamental principle that underlies the development of any ministry: never call a ministry forth until a system of support is firmly in place. If taken seriously, this rule would mean that for every known ministry a congregation supports, someone should be praying for the one who ministers and for those whose lives are touched. In addition, at some time during the year someone should ask this person how it is going and be prepared to listen to the response with care and interest. There has been a lot of emphasis in recent years on the ministry of the whole church—clergy and laity together. Ministry development in the local church has bogged down or become misdirected where a trained system of support is lacking.

Prayer and ministry are two sides of the same coin, for ministry is nothing less than our outward expression of our inner identity in Christ. Ministry is deepened as the life of Christ is deepened, and that happens through worship and a rhythm of intercession and action that allows one's inner life to be nourished.

In a provocative comment made during the heart of the peace protests during the 1960s Thomas Merton wrote:

> To allow one's self to be carried away by a multitude of conflicting concerns, to surrender to too many demands, to commit oneself to too many projects, to want to help everyone in everything is to succumb to violence. Frenzy destroys our inner capacity for peace. It destroys the fruitfulness of our work, because it kills the root of inner wisdom which makes work fruitful.[9]

Where ministries of counsel flourish, there are ministries of spiritual companionship and direction to support them. You cannot have one without the other. Ministries of spiritual counsel are ministries aimed at helping others deepen their life in Christ. If a crisis ministry is geared to help people find the inner strength and energy to go on with their lives, ministries of spiritual direction are geared to making the life of prayer an available and usable resource.

### The Pastor as Counselor

In any congregation the quality of pastoral care depends largely on the energy, skill, and wisdom of the priest or pastor who bears the responsibility for the congregation's well-being. The pastor's energy for the task is closely related to his or her vocational motivation and sense of well-being. The wisdom we need as pastors is a gift that comes through our encounter with the Spirit in the deepest aspects of our lives. Skill we can learn, and must learn, if the church is to flourish.

Many centuries ago, Irenaeus described a priest as the burden bearer of the people of God. A priest or pastor, in his understanding, was one who willingly took on the burdens of others in order to call others to this ministry and to help people experience the limitless compassion and wisdom of

Christ. Paul wrote to the Galatians: "Bear one another's burdens, and in this way you will fulfill the law of Christ [Gal. 6:2]." The calling of the ordained person is so to reflect the love of Christ in his or her own life that what is seen and experienced is an invitation to others to share in the burden bearing of Jesus. It is an awesome invitation indeed—an invitation impossible to fulfill, if it were not for the fact that in Christ the weight of every burden we carry can be transformed into a source of strength and possibility. It is this miracle of transformation, empowered by the Spirit of God, that makes the counseling ministry of the church a source of wisdom and hope and holiness without which society would be bereft indeed.

## CHAPTER 2

# Sermons as Instruments of Care and Counseling

## Samuel Southard

IN ONE VOLUME OF THE *Communicators Commentary*, Bruce Larsen describes a time when he gave helium balloons to every worshiper in a staid Presbyterian church. He exhorted the congregation to release the balloons at any time during the service when they had a strong sense of joy. By the close of the service, one third of the congregation were still holding on to their balloons.

When my wife, Donna, read this illustration she said, "Why of course, they're saving them for their grandchildren!"

Larsen had issued a proclamation—Presbyterians do not know how to be joyous. Donna had given an explanation— Presbyterians cannot be joyous because they postpone gratification.

It's the explanation of attitude and behavior that brings pastoral counseling into the pulpit. But once the explanation is a part of the sermon, it is more than a psychological insight. Human reasoning is made part of the ultimate meaning of

**Samuel Southard**, Ph.D., is professor of pastoral theology at Fuller Theological Seminary, Pasadena, California.

life. Our attempts to explain ourselves begin to make sense as part of a divine-human drama, which is our continual disorder and God's faithful design for our redemption.

In biblical terms the combination of proclamation with explanation is called wisdom. Wisdom is our willingness to affirm God's purposes for creation despite our knowledge of rebellion, selfishness, despair, and deceit. This is the realistic hope with which Job defies his comforters.

> But I would speak to the Almighty,
>     and I desire to argue my case with God.
> As for you, you whitewash with lies;
>     all of you are worthless physicians.
> If you would only keep silent,
>     that would be your wisdom!
>
> —Job 13:3–6

In the midst of self-deceived counselors, Job pours out his explanations of human suffering—only to be contradicted and accused by another "miserable comforter [Job 16:2]."

The continual dialogue of divine hope and human deceit provides the context of pastoral counsel in a sermon. As we pastors proclaim God's truth, we are wisely aware that words are used both to reveal and to conceal who we are before God.

Wisdom has us ask two questions about our preaching: What is the capacity of these people to receive the truth about themselves and God at this time of their individual lives? How is my presentation of the truth about God and self conditioned by my own character and my need for security and recognition here and now?

How do we as pastors explain ourselves and others when these questions condition our message? The wisdom literature of the Bible offers us four resources: (1) international intelligence, (2) moral guidance, (3) prophetic insight, and (4) the incarnation of wisdom in Christ (Isa. 9:6; 1 Cor. 1:24).

### International Intelligence

On the day Donna made her observation about Presbyterians saving for their grandchildren, I listened to a well-known Presbyterian pastor on television. His sermon was based on five principles of the Puritan work ethic. After announcing his subject, he issued a warning that a secular, spending society had brought us to the place where we expect our grandchildren to take care of our present and future needs. He spoke with horror of this reversal of expectations. This would not have been a time for Bruce Larsen to give out helium balloons. Probably not one of them would have been released.

The Puritan work ethic is an example of international intelligence. The intelligence is composed of culturally conditioned truths that form the subfloor of many sermons. In popular, secular terminology this is "wisdom." Wise counsel is based on prudent, considered experience and competent action in one or more cultures to live decently with others and to master the various problems of life and life itself. It is the first building block of wisdom in Proverbs:

> For learning about wisdom and instruction,
>    for understanding words of insight,
> for gaining instruction in wise dealing
>    righteousness, justice, and equity.
> —Proverbs 1:2–3

G. Ernest Wright refers to these sayings as "international intelligence" because they function as wise sayings in several nations and fit the needs of a wide variety of peoples.[1] They also represent the accumulation over time of responses to varied crises in the lives of leaders and nations.

International intelligence may be displayed in two ways. First, we are wise to follow collections of tested experience to which wise people have given common assent. This is characteristic of the book of Proverbs. Aphorisms are presented in a way that might meet varying needs: "To watch over mouth and tongue is to keep out of trouble [Prov. 21:23]." These collections of tested experiences for the solutions of life's problems form traditional guidebooks that serve more as stimuli to reflection than as final answers, since varying viewpoints on the same subject may be found in any collection of commonsense sayings.

The second way international intelligence is displayed is in the use of individual sagacity in solving interpersonal problems. Solomon is extolled for this type of wisdom (1 Kings 3:16–28; 10:1–3). Prophets look forward to a ruler of this quality: "The spirit of the LORD shall rest on him, the spirit of wisdom and understanding. . . . He shall not judge by what his eyes see or decide by what his ears hear [Isa. 11:2–3]." He will not judge by appearance or hearsay.

The Gospels present Jesus' way of thinking with sagacity and prudence as one of the attributes that drew people to him or preserved his integrity under attack:

- realistic observations (the way Pharisees predict weather, Matt. 16:1–4; the way hypocrites fast, Matt. 6:16–19)
- practical classification (the condition of soil before planting is like varying conditions of readiness to hear the Gospel, Matt. 13:10–17)
- concise explanations (some Pharisees will not believe the healing of a blind man because it is a judgment upon their blindness, John 9:39–41)

How do these two aspects of international intelligence increase a pastor's capacity to explain to an audience their reasons for accepting or rejecting the truth about God and ourselves?

*Common Assumptions and the Reduction of Anxiety*

The first teaching of wisdom about international intelligence is that common assumptions about wisdom will reduce anxiety whenever a pastor presents some incisive truth. An example is a sermon preached in a small Texas church by Wesley Deats when he was a student at the Institute of Religion in 1955. Civil rights legislation was very controversial, and Deats was urging his congregation to change their attitudes of approval of racial segregation. He began by saying: "I'm not talking this morning about what happens in a state university when an intelligent black man applies for admission. I'm talking about you and me when we are out in the field with a big black buck and think about drinking out of the same water pail and sitting together at lunch with the other threshers." Deats reported that his sermon was heard with respect, even though it was a respectful silence. He "had" them because he was "one of them."

The power of international intelligence is in the universality of the illustrations. Both preacher and audience should look out upon the world or into themselves through the same window. One of the most appealing examples of this resource is the sermons of Peter Marshall, who continually referred to scenes of his Scottish homeland in sermons at the New York Avenue Presbyterian Church in Washington, D.C., after World War II.

But how well do those illustrations fit the post-Vietnam generations? Part of my sabbatical research in 1986 was a study of the ministry of Orange County, California, churches to singles. More than 50 percent of the adults in Orange County were single. More than 50 percent of the children who entered first grade in the county were from single-parent families. At the same time, only 9 percent of the people met the ideal of a Christian family that was presented from pulpits in the county, on religious television, and in books on marriage and the family. This ideal was a married couple who had never been divorced and who would be together for life. The husband was successful in his work and was emotionally supported by the wife, who found her identity through her husband and enjoyed caring for at least two children at home. Both children were from the same parents.

This 9 percent was the focus of whatever "international intelligence" was presented on adult identity and relationships from Orange County pulpits. What about the other 91 percent? One pastor told all the divorced people of the congregation that they were sinners who must make confession and return to their former spouses. Another announced in a business meeting that a successful man could now be a candidate for deacon because he had recently married. A third tried hard to include singles in his program announcements but failed to do so until he caught my eye in the audience and added, "We'd like all the singles to come to this church picnic also." There were illustrations about children, mothers, fathers, husbands, wives. Usually there were no references to the divorced, the widows or widowers, the unmarried, or the spouses, who felt like second-class citizens.

It was certainly a testimony to the reconciling power of the Spirit to find that some congregations were 10 percent or 20 percent single adults. These singles were an invisible people, very much like the "dark people" who made up 90 percent of the Russian population before the 1917 revolution. So far as I could tell from either the content or the illustrations of sermons, they did not exist except on those occasions when church discipline or morality shed a glaring light on their supposed failures. As one pastor said on a Sunday morning: "Since I'm preaching through the Gospels, I have to deal this morning with the next chapter, Matthew 19, in which there is a reference to divorce. I would never talk on this subject if it were not right here in the Bible and I hope that I will never have to mention it again." He denounced those who were divorced, and as a result a number of recently remarried people left the church. One of his staunch supporters commented to me several weeks later: "I don't know why they took offense. They were good workers in the church. I'm sure he was not talking about them." My conclusion was that the pastor accepted the part of them labeled "good workers" because that success-oriented category was the only window through which he could see people. A failure, like divorce, would block out that window. The 91 percent were accepted in his church *if* their failures were never known.

Wisdom requires the impact of any culture upon "the little ones," the failures, the minorities. The impact causes continual tension between being "in the world" and not being "of the world." The biblical solution to this tension is to recognize our selfish and hedonistic tendency to restrict international intelligence to the foolish worship of mortal sensations and fantasies (Rom. 1:18–23). This proud and callous view of the world is denounced by Paul as the "world's wisdom" (1 Cor. 1:20–25).

A pithy proverb issues the same warning: "Do not be wise in your own eyes; fear the LORD and turn away from evil. [Prov. 3:7]."

## The Wisdom of God as a Challenge to Tradition

The second teaching of wisdom about international intelligence is that the wisdom of God challenges the accumulated traditions of a particular culture. We are to recognize the injustice of any culture that will not change to meet the needs of those who are deprived or depressed. The idealized illustrations of one generation can be read as signs of rejection by the next.

How do we as pastors explain our responses to this challenge? I think of cultural wisdom as a necessary but restricting view of who we are as human beings. We continually see ourselves in the light of idealized images of the saint, the hero, the wise man of our culture.

Notice the reference to wise *man*. That's my conditioning. Autonomous, independent, self-reliant thought was a goal in my sermon preparation. By way of contrast, did I confer with others in the development of a theme, or give illustrations that showed my interdependence with others? Not until very recently. I was a *man* of God. I conferred with the writings of other white power males.

Even the structures of the sermons were masculine. They often began with definitions. I sought exactness in exegesis. A logical accumulation of arguments toward some central truth was followed by the call for a clear-cut, independent decision. Where were the flow of feeling, the sense of mystery, the awareness of limitations, the willingness to look for others who would lead me in time toward deeper truth? They were not there because I thought I was wise enough with the parts of myself that I would admit I possessed. But it was very incomplete knowledge of self and it ignored both the shadow and the feminine in me and in my message.[2]

I still have trouble with this balance, as you may see in the organization of this essay. Because I couldn't really acknowledge culturally repressed parts of myself, my sermons were not really friendly. Why do I come to this conclusion? Because I recognize how Jesus defined friendship: "I have called you friends, because I have made known to you everything that I have heard from my Father [John 15:15]."

I wouldn't admit how God had really made me or the messages sent to me about the feminine and the shadow side of myself. If I had permitted deeper knowledge of myself, I would have had more insightful messages for others who were like me and I would have admitted some of the ways in which we were different. Paul explains: "Here we are, then, speaking for Christ, as though God himself were making his appeal through us. We plead on Christ's behalf: let God change you from enemies into his friends [2 Cor. 5:20, TEV]!"

So long as part of ourselves is an enemy, our appeal for Christ will not be friendly. This is an essential insight to work through in preaching that includes explanations. By "work through" I mean a process of moral understanding that leads us deeper into ourselves as God originally created us. Do we see and know how to follow God's guidelines for life?

## Moral Guidance

An accurate sensitivity to the way that we pastors think and the way that others respond is one essential element of counsel in the proclamation of God's word. The need to be bold and understanding with these personal insights in the midst of a conforming culture has just been discussed. But more is required than a general analysis of dehumanizing trends. Pastoral preaching also requires an explanation of individual motivation. Why do people in any culture deceive themselves and manipulate others? Why do people hide from each other in the midst of their pain and project responsibility for their problems upon others who hardly know them?

The biblical resource for meeting this challenge is an affair of the heart. This is the deeper way to the wisdom of God in the midst of disobedience and deception: "Who has felt the full power of your anger? Who knows what fear your fury can bring? Teach us how short our life is, so that we may become wise [Ps. 90:11-12 TEV]."

Emotional depth of understanding will lead to loving compassion and righteous action:

> Mak[e] your ear attentive to wisdom
>     and inclin[e] your heart to understanding;
> . . . cry out for insight.
> For the LORD gives wisdom;
> . . . Then you will understand
> righteousness and justice, . . .
>     every good path;
> for wisdom will come into your heart,
>     and knowledge will be pleasant to your soul.
>             —Proverbs 2:2–10.

The passions of the soul united with the power of God produce apt discernment and finely tuned discretion in decisions (Isa. 28:28–29).

Fine tuning is necessary because there are different degrees of personal deceit and misinterpretation of the truth in each person, generation, section of the country, or social class. In the 1890s deception in preacher and people could be traced to excessive identification with the noble emotional repression characteristic of Robert E. Lee or Queen Victoria. In the 1980s such deception usually had no moral model, and impulsive adaptation to any thrilling moment numbed anxiety and pain.

This challenge to clarity of emotional understanding is almost bewildering when pastors are preaching in a changing culture to people of several generations. The recent experience that Donna and I had as part-time pastors to young adult singles in West Hollywood, California, demonstrates my sympathy with this problem. I was a sixty-year-old Southerner with a Baptist and Presbyterian background, in the midst of young Californians who had never heard of John Wesley, John Calvin, Martin Luther, or Stonewall Jackson. They were just "going straight" after years on drugs, forming support groups to help them out of a gay lifestyle, or confessing or denying their hatred of men who had seduced them.

At the center of their anguishing circumstances we saw two major problems: deceit and secrecy. These people wanted the emotional release of general confessions during periods of group prayer, but they did not want specific acknowledgment of the trouble that their twisted way of thinking had caused. They wanted support, guidance, and warm fellowship without confrontation of their flaky, irresponsible attitudes and admission of their overdependence upon others. They lived in a world of black-and-white morality, continually denouncing themselves and others concerning sex and drugs but never in such a way that their own secrecy, deceit, and unrealistic outlook would be questioned.

So how did Donna and I reach the heart of the matter with such a congregation? How did we keep the promises of wisdom to reach the depths of a secretive soul who is really more deprived than depraved? We decided to speak plainly about personal problems, provide biblical guidance, and give people a chance to talk about the impact of the sermon in fifteen minutes of open discussion near the close of the service and in more intense examination during prayer groups after the benediction.

I would like to have my readers' evaluation of my sermonic attempts to deal specifically with secrecy and deceit, but before they ask to see my sermon files I should admit that more than half the congregation was gone after one year of these sermons.

Why then should I recommend open moral counsel before a congregation that is embedded in deceit and secrecy? For one thing, I learned a lot about myself and about people who are different from me in some ways and like me in others. I found that I could not preach effectively in a congregation of co-dependents (that is, pairs of people who have an unhealthy dependence on substances and on each other) unless I used illustrations that were very personal and penetrating. Nothing could be taken for granted. Also, I began to appreciate the reassuring messages in sermons preached in a particular section of the South which I was studying in the 1960s. At first I thought the Southern minister was protecting the people by giving them peace of mind and predigested solutions to the general problems of life. But after my experience in West Hollywood I realized that the Californian ministers were reassuring themselves more than anyone else. They needed to feel effective. So long as their messages did not come too close to the deeper levels of the soul, the congregations accepted them, and a convenient bargain was struck. Ministers will be rewarded for preaching in those areas of life where the congregation is willing to listen.

Sooner or later we should honestly admit the limits of our security in preaching. Donna and I faced that when the restlessness of the congregation became intense. People told me that they knew I had the gift of healing and that they would feel the power of the Holy Spirit in my messages if I would just do some signs and wonders. Others said that I should stop quoting scripture for each point of my sermon and let the Spirit carry me away with power to denounce sin. The most generous financial contributor to the congregation wanted a white light to flood his soul each Sunday and cleanse him from "kinky" sexual thoughts that obsessed him every day in his office.

Out of compassion for people who had found some emotional security in a rather loosely structured fellowship, Donna and I thought of backing off and trying to find some "white light" that would give general satisfaction, but we didn't. Was it because I had a tenured position at a seminary and only preached on the weekends? Was it my "hard headedness"? I don't know, but I am aware that an open discussion of the problems of co-dependence can be risky, both to the congregation and to the preacher.[3]

### Prophetic Insight

My failure to produce a "white light" each Sunday in West Hollywood may illustrate the need for every preacher to be a prophet. In one way the prophetic function of preaching points the way by which moral power may come to the congregation. Individuals are empowered when they belong to a social unit where righteousness is dominant. As ministers, we call people out of isolation and selfishness into a community that prizes justice and mercy for all. In another way the prophetic function of preaching is related to the psychological issues of counseling. This function is the faculty of feeling what others are feeling, the ability to see individuals in their future as well as their present state, and the ability to show how present attitudes will have future consequences.

The outcome of prophetic wisdom is insight that persists. The prophet foresees the unfolding of the interdependent consequences of deep motives, consequences that may only dimly be perceived in the souls of the individual or the group at the present time. Interpreting the shadowy outline of things to come, the prophet counsels action and attitudes that will fulfil the will of God as God has made people to function as individuals, families, tribes, and cultures. (For an example of this function, see the words of Jeremiah against the puppet king Zedekiah in Jeremiah 38:22–23.)

It takes time for this preaching to be called prophetic preaching. At first it will be called psychology, meddling, or worldliness. Why? Because the pastoral function of prophetic preaching is to expose the defensive detachment of people from the way that God has created them to be with God and one another. The exposure is accepted as helpful if the preacher predicts the consequences of a person's way of thinking in such a way that the person can observe them in the self or in others and can make sense out of them. It is to be hoped that there will be enough trust and truth flowing between pastor and people for them to gain a gradual aware-ness of insightful prophecy. Paul describes the outcome of this prophetic work: the secrets of the heart will be disclosed, and the unbeliever or outsider will declare that God is really among these people (1 Cor. 14:24–25). True prophetic com-munication brings self-insight and eventual change.

How do we as pastors present insight that persists? We can offer explanations that stimulate self-reflection and contrast human disorder with God's redemptive design for life. I tried to do this in a sermon that uncovered the deprivations of love from which many in the congregation suffered and described the destructive ways in which they reacted to the deprivation. The sermon was entitled "Blessed or Bitchy?" and was based on Matthew 5:4 and 2 Corinthians 7:5–11. I asked why the grieving of some persons made them bitchy while others passed through sorrow with blessings.

My first point was that the death of any dream saps our energy and leaves us dull. The death may be a physical loss, the rupture of an intimate relationship, a devastating change of environment, a betrayal of hope, a disappointment or rage against rampant injustice. I noted that there were many signs of chronic mourning in the congregation. Members showed the morbid grief that binds energy in a tight spiral of pity, rage, frustration, and helplessness. Although our members were relatively young, they seemed to have little available energy to sing heartily, show up on time, or remember events that were not absolutely necessary for their existence. They could be described by this quote: "Like mourners we force ourselves to greet people; we sit in self-imposed sorrow and wait for others to notice us." We are drained of life, I explained, so long as we cannot admit our sorrow and find the source. Instead, some of us alternate between unimaginative despair and a rush for a substitute in a "hype" experience.

Second, I suggested that we recognize enough of these deadening symptoms to make us seek the alternative, which is godly sorrow. Such sorrow would be admission of our depleted condition, willingness to look openly at our hurts, and submission to a new center of power in our life from God, which would replace the self-imposed sadness that now drains our energy.

Third, I asked how we may begin godly sorrow. We will not come to it until we have had time to examine with others the questions that reveal our earlier griefs. I asked the congregation to meet in groups of five or six for fifteen minutes to discuss three questions: What loss has affected you most in the past few years? Is there some earlier loss that shows itself? What are the signs that we have been blessed as we move through mourning? Then I asked the congregation to take the questions and answers to heart during the following week and talk to one another about what they were beginning to learn. The service closed with a benediction and an invitation to those who desired prayer to come forward.

Prophetic insight begins to work when pastors offer their people some concepts, some words and phrases that explain what they are feeling. As one person said after worshiping with us from some time: "You are right when you say that you can't really feel everything that has happened to us—you're older and came out of a more secure age. But you're trained to describe what we feel. You give me words to identify what's happened to me. That's power. And you point to alternatives which I never thought of before."

Deprived people don't listen well the first time pastors use a word that really describes their condition—at least they don't really know what to do with the word-feeling combination right away. Also, they have myriad defenses against change that resourceful people do not clutch quite so strongly. Why should they change? they ask. Nothing ever worked before. Besides, they have rearranged reality internally in order to enjoy neurotic satisfactions. Whatever substitute for joy they have in life depends upon their invulnerability to change. They are paralyzed by inner conflicts, fear, and anxiety.

So pastors have to recognize the need of deprived people to remain the same, note the anger that some feel as sermons and group discussions expose their defenses, and remain faithful to prophetic insight despite the cries of some that we are not "moving in signs and wonders."

I guess that my tenacity was fueled by a desire to heal. I become quite aggressive around co-dependent people who use religion to mask their ineptness. I've learned not to condemn them but to be tenacious in my observations and presentation of alternatives. I don't think that I had much love for some of our members, and I'm not sure that I always spoke the truth in love and self-control; but I do know that love and truth are the most powerful assault weapons against deceit and secrecy in deprived people. And we are all deprived in some way.

So I was tenacious. In sermon after sermon I returned to the themes of deceit, denial, and secrecy as barriers to an abundant life with others and God. This emphasis was coupled with an admission that my sermons were immediately rearranged by deprived and depressed people to fit their personal concepts of self and others. I suggested that this rearrangement of reality was necessary to maintain their satisfaction with many forms of addiction: religious, sexual, alcoholic, drug, eating, and spending. My work as teacher was to point out the signs of these defenses so often that a person would eventually say, "This makes sense. I would not continually harm and defeat myself in the way that I do unless I had developed an invulnerable screen against reality." When a person has said this, I pray that he or she will admit, "This is a power game that I want to give up, but I will need divine strength to tear down the walls that separate me from myself and from others and God."

I would often show that I appreciated how a substitute satisfaction could keep persons permanently disabled. In some way the substitutes must seem good to them. Could I present the mind of Christ as an attractive alternative to these secret, self-defeating satisfactions?

## Christ the Wisdom of God

People will credit a preacher with wisdom when his or her insights begin to make sense over a period of time. Making sense over time has always been the accreditation of a prophet. He or she is believed when that which has been dimly foreseen in words of wisdom becomes historical reality that all can observe.

The New Testament presents Christ as the faithful fulfillment of God's wisdom (Heb. 1:1–3). What he said and did was the ultimate development of the divine will in human experience. He united the power and wisdom of God (1 Cor. 1:24). In passages that speak directly to co-dependent, obsessive people, the apostle Paul contrasts the power and wisdom of God in Christ with the "lofty words of wisdom" of the Corinthians (1 Cor. 2:1). He traces the distortions caused by self-deception and interpersonal divisiveness in those who justify their immaturity with showy gifts and instant spirituality.

In contrast to the protective system of these "uninformed" people (1 Cor. 12:1), Paul presents honest admission of faults, and dedication to purposes beyond ourselves, with risk and joyous commitment to a fellowship sustained by friendship. The model is Jesus' sharing with the disciples on the night of his betrayal. He knew they would flee for a time, but he loved them confidently (11:18–34). This is the "excellent way" (12:31) toward an understanding of the self in the light of God's love (13:13). In contrast, the secretive and self-deceived Corinthians offered powerful associations, angelic talk, mountain-moving faith, extractive relationships, and perpetual assertions of autonomy (13:1–6). To Paul, we gain nothing through these exercises because they only edify the performer (14:4). His joy and approval are for the prophet who is motivated by love for all the congregation and a desire to see that all speak clearly concerning themselves and God (14:1–5). Earlier, Paul warned that those who do not "discern the body" during the Lord's Supper will grow sick and die (11:29–30).

So, in Paul's analysis of deception, the basic decision people must make is between life and death. This is a horrible contrast for obsessive and co-dependent people to hear through a sermon or anywhere else. Their greatest fear is that they are not really alive, which indeed they are not. The driving force of their addictions is a temporary feeling of being alive through consuming drugs or alcohol, displaying showy spiritual gifts, indulging in compulsive sexual practices, or practicing weekly religiosity. They cannot wait for the magical moment on Saturday night when someone will come up to them in a bar and say, "You're beautiful, I love you. What's your name?," or the purging experience of a "white light" that makes them clean for a moment on Sunday morning.

We are often preaching to people engaged in a slowly draining dance with death. The paradox of our message is that they must die to their false selves if they are going to live as God intended God's sons and daughters to live through Jesus Christ.

How can we deal compassionately and courageously with this paradox through our sermons? I suggest the method that I see in 1 Corinthians, where Paul identifies substitutes for spiritual life and then presents the living and growing alternative in Christ. The particular substitutes that we see in one congregation will not be exactly those of another. Let me use the work in West Hollywood as one example of preaching that may make the sacrifice of a substitute seem worthwhile in return for a freer life in Christ.

### Frozen Feelings

One substitute for a full life is frozen feelings. I told the obsessive congregation that this was their protection against the overwhelming fear of disapproval. They were continually saying to themselves, "If people really knew what I am like, they would not like me." This is the way a secret desire can remain dominant over them, I warn them. If it were shared, in a Christian fellowship, then it would lose power because people approve of the person who can share both strengths and weaknesses. The obsessive person will think that such sharing will cause death and rejection. In some places in the past this would probably have been so, but persons will testify today that it is not true in our congregation. So who, I ask, will take a chance and die to the idolatrous self in order to gain full life here and hereafter? We can see in Christ that the human feelings of anger, grief, disappointment, and anguish can be expressed without sin. Why then do we try to be more Christian than Christ?

### Perfectionism

A second substitute that brings satisfaction to many addictive people is perfectionism. I addressed this subject in a sermon called "The Right Start in Life" based on Matthew 3:13–17. I stressed openness before God, openness with the self, and openness with others. On the last point, I expounded Paul's teaching in Romans 5:8 that the righteousness of Christ was fulfilled in his identification with our unrighteousness. In contrast I described people's temptation to be an exception to unrighteousness, to hope that they won't be like other humans who fail, falsify, fear, and die. These overwhelming fears lead to a postponement of commitments because involvement in life would bring compromises. As involved people we are likely to be working with others who are imperfect or infectious. We may be agreeing to decisions that are not as exact and timely as we would desire; we may have to abandon some of our habits and preferences because they will be a stumbling block to people who do not think exactly as we think.

Why, I ask, do we think that our salvation will come through this compelling desire to look good, act without mistakes, and win universal approval? Christ died for us just as we are, unrighteous. Perhaps this is why we do not feel his love because we have never felt love as an unrighteous person. We have always been told that we must obey in a certain way or attain a certain success to gain the approval of parents and other important people. So how can we feel that anyone would die for us as we really are in our imperfections? I then ask that members of the congregation test out this question with one another. Who has ever been really accepted as a human without some strings attached? How did each person respond to that manipulation and exploitation in the past? How does each of us respond now?

## Dishonesty

The challenge of these questions cannot be answered without giving some attention to the third substitute for the full life, dishonesty. I described dishonesty as a coping strategy for some children to survive in dysfunctional families. Parents explain away family secrets or hide them. As children we learn to avoid these pressure points in the mind field of deception and soon avoid pressure points in ourselves.

How then can we detect dishonesty in ourselves and others? The signs are usually alternation between boredom and temporary excitement. The boredom is a symptom of emotional deprivation in primary interpersonal contacts. We cannot talk with others about the things that really matter to either one of us. The temporary excitement is a way to express some feeling without having to take responsibility for who we really are. We go to a singles bar to begin anonymous sex, or we go to a crowded religious meeting in another part of town where no one will ask any intimate questions when we let a secret emotion overpower us.

The dishonesty will not die, I warn, until we have the courage to admit there is still some life in us. We are not totally possessed by our internal substitutes for life. Our will must cooperate with God's will to break through the terror of self-discovery. We cannot crawl to the cross. We must have enough confidence to stand up before we can kneel down before our Savior. Christ believed enough in us to die for us. Why can't we believe enough in ourselves to call our helplessness and hopelessness a lie?

## The Impact of Insight

What is the impact of persistent insight on obsessive, depleted people? One person who left the West Hollywood church had this analysis of the sermons: "You're trying to tell me that the basic problem is not what I do, but how I think. You say that is a defense against change. Well, I think that's a good point, but I need more power than your psychologizing provides. I'm going to a church that is filled with the Holy Spirit. I can *see* immediate change in those people that you only talk about."

In one way he's right. Only the power of the Holy Spirit can show up these substitutes for what they really are and detonate the defensive system of an obsessive person from within. I had said that many times from the pulpit, but my life and that of many in the congregation must not have impressed him. Some others were impressed and indignantly proclaimed in his presence the changes they had seen in themselves and others over the period of a year. He listened politely and eventually drifted away. They had talked about self-confidence, honesty, acceptance of limitations, and the ability to express feelings without fear. He did not see those as the fruit of the Spirit. His soul was set upon the tree in the Garden of Eden that would give him absolute knowledge of good and evil. Then he would have the protection of spiritual perfection. He would no longer be a self shattered by the shame of his former homosexual behavior and would never have to be tested for the AIDS virus.

I shared with others the sorrow of this man's departure, but we were not really comforted when he returned fleetingly to our "gay rap group" to tell us of his numerous experiences of healing. Yet in a way I felt that his attitude helped me to relax in my preaching. I really was not going to reach anyone without a combination of both power that I could not control and wisdom that was beyond my understanding. So I just did my best with the gifts that I had and urged the congregation that they should do the same.

That's the story of some preaching by a pastoral counselor in one small congregation. It certainly was not a success in terms of church growth, but it was very satisfying. I learned from my Bible study and conversations with Donna and the congregation to rejoice in my specific strengths and live with my weaknesses.

From the pulpit I was gradually developing the context for wisdom, which was a congregation in which we could worship as friends. Christ told all he knew from the Father to his friends, and his Spirit gives his followers the wisdom and power for open commitment. We feel with others that it is no shame to be a broken self. Our need is not invulnerable perfection but love and truth to overcome the deceit and secrecy that prevent healing.

## CHAPTER 3

# The Moral Context of Counseling

## James B. Nelson

I DID NOT PICK THE TITLE FOR THIS ESSAY, BUT I AM QUITE satisfied with it. As an ethical contextualist, I am understandably happy with the word *context*. Webster's two definitions are these: first, context is the parts of a sentence or paragraph surrounding a particular word or passage and determining its exact meaning; second, context is the background or environment relevant to a particular event or person. Accordingly, this essay will consider some moral realities, backgrounds, and environments surrounding counseling and giving it meaning. My one revision to the title would be a slight but important addition—the letter "s." Instead of the singular, let us speak of several moral contexts for counseling.

### Four Overlapping Circles

Consider now four moral contexts. They are overlapping, interconnected, contextual circles, and they are, I believe, inescapable in counseling.

James B. Nelson, Ph.D., is professor of Christian ethics at the United Theological Seminary at the Twin Cities, Minneapolis.

The first context is that *the fundamental purpose of counseling is a moral one*. To put it simply, the purpose is to help make right something that has gone wrong. The parishioner or client comes with a problem (it might even be said that the person is "demoralized"), and the counselor helps the individual to move into a different way of understanding his or her life situation, a fresh way of defining what is or is not desirable, and, it is to be hoped, a greater ability to realize something new. As contextualists like to insist, the real stuff of ethics is not principles or rules, ideas or abstractions, but relationships. Counseling is one important mode of dealing with wounded, broken, or underdeveloped relationships with others, with God, and with the self. So, the basic reason for counseling and the "stuff" of which it is composed constitutes a moral context.

The second context is *the theological-ethical commitments in the counseling method itself*. Whether done by clergy or secular practitioners, counseling is necessarily based on some interpretations of the purpose of life, the causes of human difficulties, and the secrets for human change. Counseling is always a religious or quasi-religious enterprise, involving some theological-ethical notions of creation, human nature, sin, and redemption. Indeed, as many have argued, the very definition of mental health itself is a profoundly religious and moral enterprise.

More specifically, for example, the influences of Carl Rogers, Abraham Maslow, and Eric Fromm have led many counselors to emphasize the importance of self-regard in helping an individual regain personal power and health. But as Paul Tillich years ago and Don Browning and numerous feminists more recently have pointed out, the place of self-regard in human life has not been the subject of just a narrow psychological debate; it has been the subject of a basic discussion of the ethical foundations of human relations and of the nature of human loving.[1]

The third moral context involves the counselor's basic

attitudes and actions regarding *respect and coercion*. If the general aim of counseling is to assist the parishioner or client in changing something—perceptions, feelings, actions—the issues of respect and coercion are always present. How much counseling is persuasion, obvious or subtle? When does the counselor know best? When is informed consent essential, and when is it truly informed and consenting? Sexuality issues enter significantly here. When and how is physical touch appropriate? The recent, much needed discussion of "the unmentionable sin," the sexual abuse of women clients by male counselors, is the obvious case in point. But sexual abuse can be subtle as well as blatant. When a counselor reinforces stereotypical, gender-defined roles or allows homophobic biases and anxieties to intrude into the counseling relationship, there are moral issues of coercion and abuse.

The fourth moral context is *the moral community*. More than ten years ago Don Browning persuasively argued that pastoral care has as a central task the incorporation of members into the meanings, goals, and distinctive lifestyles of the church.[2] To focus pastoral care or counseling simply on handling individual crises or interpersonal strains is to neglect the moral community itself and is to capitulate to an individualistic, secular, therapeutic ideology. The church is a bearer of a moral worldview; it is a place for moral discourse and decision making. Pastoral counseling is thus founded on a whole context of moral meanings, values, and norms expressing the religious community's best lights regarding how life ought faithfully to be lived—in economics and politics, in families and interpersonal relations, in environmental responsibilities, and all the rest. Pastoral counseling takes seriously the integration of the individual into the lifestyle of a faith community.

Here, then, are four moral contexts for pastoral counseling. Do not see them as "levels" in any hierarchical sense. Rather, visualize them as overlapping contextual circles, each implying the other and all having significance.

## The Spirit-Body Dualism

Now, consider the one particular moral issue that traverses all these circles. Like all moral issues, it is theological as well. It is an issue frequently neglected in counseling. Its significance is sometimes missed even by pastoral counselors committed to an incarnationalist faith. The issue is *the body*.

Most of us have known times when we felt at one with our bodies. Then we felt vibrant and alive, sensually at one with our surroundings. We had little sense of separation between the selves that we are and the bodies that we are. There was little feeling of living in a temporary home, little sense of bodily deadness, shame, or pain. Unlike St. Francis, who preferred to call his body Brother Ass, our bodies and our souls felt one, harmonious, and integrated. We were secure and at home in the world.

But those times have been too few, too fleeting, too fragmentary. In fact, we often do not realize how "dead" parts of our bodies are. We become accustomed to our tensions, our pains, our lack of bodily sensation. They have become so much part of us that they seem natural. How did this alienation of the self from the body come about? Our histories live in and through our bodies. It is true for each individual embodying his or her unique history. The "type A" coronary patient and the person struggling with anorexia or bulimia are only more noticeable examples of what is true about us all.

Our shared religious histories continue to live in us bodily, also. Both Judaism and Christianity are at once rich and ambiguous in attitudes toward the body. The Hebrews had a remarkable sense of the unity of the human being. Nowhere does the Old Testament portray the person as simply a soul inhabiting a body or the body as merely a housing for the soul. Indeed, the Hebrews frequently used various parts of the body—the heart, the kidney, the bowels—as symbols for the whole self. There was no sharp separation between the meanings of health and salvation.

Likewise, Christianity at its best conveyed a profoundly positive conviction about bodily life. Heirs of the strong Hebrew doctrine of creation, Christians also centered their faith on an incarnational claim. "In the beginning was the Word, and the Word was with God, and the Word was God [John 1:1]." And when the Word came to dwell with us it became what? A book? A creed? A theological system? A moral code? No—though some still find this embarrassing—the Word became flesh. Such was the incarnational claim. Yet, the attitudes of early Christians were also deeply affected by the cultures and social environments in which they lived. And Christianity was born into the Graeco-Roman world, a world profoundly affected by late Hellenistic dualism.

This dualism pitted spirit or soul over against body, mind over against matter. As is true of any Western dualism—and the spirit-body split may be dualism's most basic form, the parent of all others—a hierarchy of virtue and control was part of it. Thus, the spirit was assumed good and immortal, while the body was believed to be the source of sin, evil, and mortality, always needing the discipline and control of the spirit. Redemption in whatever form was escape from the body's bondage into the higher life of mind or spirit. If the Hebrews knew little of this philosophy, they knew a great deal of the companion dualism, patriarchy, which early Christians also largely embraced. Adopting both dualisms, men believed themselves essentially determined by spirit and mind and assumed women to be essentially material; therefore, men concluded that as higher beings they rightly controlled women as lower beings.

This philosophy was unevenly absorbed by Christianity. Creationism and incarnationalism could never rest easy with either a Neoplatonic dualism or with a patriarchal worldview. But the contradictions and uneasy alliances had made their inroads. And we Christians, mind and body, live with them today.

### "Our Bodies: Ourselves"

The subsequent chapters of the religious history of our body are fascinating and mixed, but they are variations on the same themes. So, let us shift our focus to contemporary psychology. Edward W. L. Smith opens his book *The Body in Psychotherapy* with these words: "The mind-body dichotomy has been so entrenched in Western thought that to consider the 'mind' to be the bailiwick of the *psycho*-therapist and the 'body' the bailiwick of the *physic*ian seems perfectly logical to most Western people."[3] I fear that there is considerable truth there. Counselors frequently focus on what is happening in the head and leave the body to the physician.

The psychotherapeutic tradition does, however, display elements of a more holistic perspective. In some ways, the founding giants recognized it. Freud observed in 1923 that the ego is "first and foremost a body-ego . . . ultimately derived from bodily sensations."[4] Mortimer Adler was long interested in the body's capacity to compensate for both physiological and psychological damage. And while Carl Jung wrote little about the body in therapy, his patients frequently danced, sang, acted, modeled with clay, and played musical instruments during treatment. Nevertheless, most of modern depth psychology continued to understand personality disorders as rooted in a disembodied mind.

But there were exceptions. Before his work lost credibility with many, Wilhelm Reich developed a significant way of seeing character as a total body phenomenon. Reich's influ-ence bore fruit in the Gestalt therapy of Fritz and Laura Perls, Franz Alexander's body therapy, Alexander Lowen's bioener-getics, and the dance therapy pioneered by Mary Starks Whitehouse, to mention a few. Indeed, a "body therapy technology" soon arose, spawning its own denominations and sects, its orthodoxies and heresies. The human potential movement picked up a good bit of this movement, and some therapists and counselors profited considerably from the experience. But the focus was heavy on practical technique, and insights into the body were not deeply probed for their religious and social significance. Even the more holistic therapists of fulfillment, such as Carl Rogers and Sidney Jourard, though well aware of the inseparable connections of body and mind, did not press a truly incarnational approach.

A more direct assault on the dualistic understandings of health came from the feminists. In the first edition (1979) of that remarkably popular book *Our Bodies, Ourselves*, fourteen members of the Boston Women's Health Collective said this of their exploration:

> The experience of learning just how little control we had over our lives and bodies, the coming together out of isolation to learn from each other in order to define what we needed, and the experience of supporting one another in demanding the changes that grew out of our developing critique—all were crucial and formative political experiences for us. . . . For us, body education is core education. Our bodies are the physical bases from which we move out into the world; ignorance, uncertainty—even, at worst, shame—about our physical selves create in us an alienation from ourselves that keeps us from being the whole people that we could be.[5]

Now, permit me a personal digression. At this point in an early draft of this essay, I was frustrated. In standard academic fashion I had come this far and had outlined further ideas I wanted to explore, but what I had sketched seemed abstract, devoid of life, cerebral. As I stared at my outline, I felt myself losing confidence that I had anything meaningful to say about the body, ethics, and counseling.

Then I reread the words from the Boston Women's Health Collective I had just typed. Immediately I was impelled to get up from my desk. I had sat there a long time. My body was numb, and my body was speaking its mind: *I* was numb. I dropped everything and went swimming—of all things— right smack in the middle of the working day. Though lap swimming is my usual exercise, this time I swam my laps more leisurely and less purposefully, and then I took a decadently long sauna. What came to me during this interlude was the conviction that I *could* be more concrete, personal, and experiential in what was to follow. For better or for worse, it was what I had to offer. And that was all right. When I returned to my desk I completely rewrote the rest of the outline.

We have reminded ourselves of some of the religious and psychological histories about the body. Now, what can we understand of the body as a moral reality in pastoral counseling? Surely, there are dimensions of the life of the body of which the counselor is usually aware. Counselors know they communicate much with clients through their own body language, and clients through their body language tell counselors a great deal about themselves and about how the therapeutic process is going. Counselors are aware of the sexual feelings that at times both they and clients experience, and of how these can affect the counseling relationship. Such body consciousness is important, indeed, but there is more to be said. Among a number of possibilities, let me suggest three interrelated moral capacities significantly rooted in body experience, capacities of enormous importance to both counselor and client: *moral understanding, compassion, and connecting*. I am a white, middle-aged male, and my own particular experience will be reflected in my illustrations of these capacities.[6]

## The Capacity for Moral Understanding

First let us consider moral understanding. I work in the field of theological ethics. Increasingly I am painfully aware of how much of Christian ethics is abstract, geared to linear logic, hyper-rationalized. Increasingly I am aware of the underdevelopment of imagination and feeling in my (male-dominated) field, yes, and in myself as a practitioner.

But here the recovery of bodily life is promising—no less for counseling than for ethics. The effective counselor draws deeply on the affective, on the imagination, on intuition, on poetic insight. The pastoral counselor no less than the ethics teacher wants to help people nurture their moral imaginations and make good decisions about their own lives and about the common good.

Though as Christians we have not yet well integrated the affective into our moral theology, the affective is deeply connected to the body. Our capacity to know what we are feeling and truly to experience those feelings is rooted in body experience. We recognize it when it is damaged or underdeveloped. Thus, the sexually abused woman may deaden her body to a large range of feelings in defense against past and future pain. And we know that, generally, men just do not have very sensitive feelings—I know what I'm thinking more clearly than what I'm feeling—a phenomenon related to men's greater alienation from their bodies. What we must yet grasp is that disconnection from the way the body feels is also disconnection from *moral* understanding, and that affective reconnection nourishes *moral* perception.

Growing up as a typical American boy, I was early conditioned to put on my armor. I learned to defend myself against all bodily attack, especially the attack on my feelings. Like many other males, I learned my lessons well. Stiff upper lip, old man. Big boys don't cry. Be a good soldier. Indeed, when at twenty-one I experienced my father's sudden death, I was literally a soldier in the army, two thousand miles away. I came home but refused to see his body in the mortuary, wanting to remember him in health not in death. And only years later did I realize how symbolic it was that I chose to attend my dad's funeral in uniform. I could not really grieve, for that would have expressed the weakness and vulnerability that I had learned to deny. It took twenty-five years and some good therapy before I could get in touch with my grief and anger. And I now know how alienated I was from a whole range of bodily feelings all those years.

My rather typical male body experience did not prepare me well to deal with death. I was uncomfortable with profound bodily changes. Women have years of submitting to the monthly menstrual cycle, over which they have little if any control. They may have experienced pregnancy, delivery, and lactation, all processes that profoundly change the body. While serious illness and accident obviously bring radical changes to some younger men, most males have matured without encountering anything comparable to the bodily transformations known by women. And death is the greatest change of all.

Like other males I tend to genitalize sexual feelings. I tend to feel my sexuality more in the genitals than in the whole erotic body and am prone to focus my sexual feeling on specific sexual acts more than upon the whole relationship. Like other males I am conditioned to sexual performance in which potency is the key sign of manhood. But in the sex act itself I experience erection, performance, and then loss of erection—life and death—while my wife can go on and on. My temporary impotence bears intimations of my mortality. No wonder French men have long called orgasm *le petit mort*, "the little death." Moreover, death seems the final threat to every cherished Western male value: invulnerability, linear progression, self-control, competition, control, mastery, winning. It is the final impotence, the fatal limpness, the utter defeat of hardness and performance. No wonder it was a male poet who urged us not to go gentle into the good night but to rage against the dying of the light.

But male alienation from bodily feelings takes a terrible toll. It leads men into abstracting themselves from the bodily concreteness and reality of others. My abstractions lure me into an exaggerated, often violent sense of reality. They entice me to lose the concreteness of the present.

After all, my physical life helps to shape my response to an often confusing world. I was conditioned by biology, religion, and society to treat my body as lower, foreign, as that which must be disciplined and controlled, as that which was irrational and must be mastered, as that which bore the intimations of decay and mortality—and that conditioning gave me a certain "feel" about the world. The world "out there" then took on some of the same confusing and half-known qualities as the body. It was full of mysterious things that smacked of badness. I needed to sort things out, to make sure that I had a clear grasp on reality. Indeed, psychologists now say that dichotomized perceptions are predictably linked with the split between mind and body. The person whose self is poorly integrated with the body likely resists ambiguity, seeking simple and single reasons for things. Then my world becomes populated with dichotomies: me/not me; masculine/feminine; heterosexual/homosexual; communist/capitalist; black/white; smart/stupid; healthy/ill; good/bad; life/death. And in the midst of all these dichotomies, the deadness of my body makes me welcome violence as a way of feeling alive again.

But these dichotomies are not the real world. The real world is richly complex, full of ambiguity, and our bodies might yet ground us in such moral sensitivity. What might ethics and pastoral care look like when counselors are more deeply connected to the tactile world of the flesh?

Think of the medical treatment of dying patients. If there are two different temptations here, one undertreatment and the other overtreatment, Western society usually chooses overtreatment. Some patients are given therapies that add little significant quality time to their lives. Indeed, many such therapies actually increase their own pain and suffering in their dying hours and hamper their communication with loved ones. True, there are many reasons for overtreatment of the dying—the attraction of applying new technologies, the fear of malpractice, guilt feelings in family members. But it is also true that frequently these problems occur simply because some of us have lost—or never have sufficiently acquired—the moral imagination that comes with bodily concreteness and feeling.

Those who press for life extension at almost any cost usually are not those who spend day after day at the dying one's bedside. They are not those who a thousand times have bathed the fevered forehead and moistened the parched lips. They are not the ones who hour after hour have massaged the restless muscles, caressed the tender skin, and viscerally know the awesome difference between an intact higher brain and a persistent vegetative state.

When these aspects of illness are not deeply known by being concretely experienced and deeply felt, abstractions take over. The patient fades into a chart and a diagnosis. Art is lost to science, and imagination's failure becomes the fear of death as an enemy to be avoided at all costs. It is no surprise that a still male-dominated medical profession is still largely a death-fearing profession. The doctor's alienation from the body becomes organized resistance to death as the final defeat.

Illustrations of lost concreteness could be multiplied. Now it is the person being counseled who becomes a diagnosis or the grieving person who is perceived as a succession of stages. The lesbian or gay individual fades into the image of a genital actor and some theories about sexual orientation. Similarly, the woman with a problem pregnancy becomes an illustration of general ethical principles.

But recovery of incarnational reality promises otherwise. It promises that we might again use abstractions in the service of flesh-and-blood life, not the other way around. (The Sabbath was made for persons, and not persons for the Sabbath.) It promises that contextual concreteness in counseling and in ethics will return. It promises that we will see freshly the relation of bodily life and moral understanding.

## The Capacity for Compassion

If the human capacity for moral understanding is bodily in many significant ways, so also is the capacity for compassion, a second incarnational reality. Webster defines "compassion" as a deep feeling of sympathy for the sufferings of another, accompanied by a strong urge to help. It is not a bad definition. For once, the dictionary is close to the biblical truth of the matter. The New Testament frequently interchanges "compassion" with "mercy." Numerous stories tell of suffering persons appealing to Jesus for mercy. These are appeals for deep sympathy, yes. They are also cries for help and healing. The Greek word describing Jesus' response is a strong term meaning literally "to be moved in one's bowels." In other words, it is to have the other's situation grab you right in the gut and to be moved viscerally to do something about it. But the notion of compassion still remains abstract until we become incarnationally concrete and put some human faces on the subject. Then let us look once more at the most dramatic and difficult challenge to the church's compassion today: Acquired Immune Deficiency Syndrome (AIDS).

It is an epidemic different from any other in our experience—unique because it is incurable in an age of high-tech medical cures, because it has been so punitively moralized, and because it fearfully links together those two greatest anxieties of Western culture, sex and death. Yes, persons with AIDS have become the biblical lepers of our time, the untouchables.

If, as scripture says, "perfect love casts out fear," the opposite is also true: fear always casts out love and compassion. We simply cannot be compassionate to those whom we deeply fear. Since our fears of AIDS are so bodily, let us look at them with the body focus. Once again I speak out of my own experience, now as a "recovering homophobic," aware that homophobia is particularly virulent among males in

Western society. Yet no one is immune from homophobia, whatever the person's gender or sexual orientation. What, then, are some of the body dynamics?

Projection, clearly, is one. We project our own unacceptable feelings onto others and then blame them for what we have been taught to reject in ourselves. A text from Mark is appropriate here (this time Mark Twain, a great American saint). Twain once said, "There are two kinds of people in the world: people who divide people into two kinds of people, and people who don't." In fact, there are not two sharply divided kinds of people regarding sexual orientation. Probably none of us is exclusively heterosexual or homosexual, particularly when variables other than genital expression are considered—erotic attraction, fantasy, emotional preference, and the preferred sex for social interaction. And all of these factors are subject to variation over our life spans. But we resist acknowledging any same-sex feelings in ourselves. And alienation from the body compounds that problem by encouraging dichotomized perceptions. So we see only either/or situations—never both/and ones. We then punish others for exemplifying too obviously what we ourselves also share but cannot acknowledge.

Envy is another body dynamic involved in homophobia. We have been taught to distrust, even despise, our own bodily sexuality. Even in enlightened adulthood, we cannot fully escape our early lurking suspicions that God somehow made a mistake and that our sexuality is an embarrassment to high-minded, "spiritual" religion. At the same time, we are angry about the shame and guilt we have absorbed for simply being sexual. We yearn for the vibrant reintegration of our sexuality with our spirituality. But homosexual stereotypes remind many of us of our deprivation. For if we identify ourselves as straight, gays and lesbians seem to be much more sexual than we are. That, after all, is the way a sexual stereotype functions. Whether the other is a butcher, baker, or candlestick maker, whether the other is Methodist, Catholic, or agnostic, is immaterial. Through stereotype I perceive the other primarily as genital actor. "They" are more sexual than I am—and that surely is cause for envy, indeed, anger.

I find the dynamic of envy particularly powerful in those of us who are male and have learned to identify ourselves as straight. As males, we have largely genitalized our sexuality and linked our manliness with potency. It is potency in bed, to be sure, but also in athletics, in work, in politics, and in life itself. But the image of the gay male as super-sexed, as forever interested and ready for "it," can give rise (in the subconscious workings of the mind) to the envy that he is more potent than I. This can be cause for rage, particularly when "manhood" for males in Western society is never fully established but forever has to be earned and proven, and then proven again.

Fear and guilt about "womanization" are additional body dynamics. In a still-sexist society, men have been taught to trivialize women, and women have been taught to trivialize themselves. But as long as sexism retains its power, a male's fear of womanization will be the virulent one. In the hierarchy of prestige and power, he is the one to lose status. Though the gay male's supposed potency makes him "more a man than I," in another way he embodies the frightening possibility of a male's womanization. After all, stereotype pictures him as one willing to be sexually passive, a receiver, one who is penetrated.

Further, the gay male threatens to womanize me in another way because I think he may see me not primarily as another person but primarily as a desired body. But that is the way heterosexual men for so long and so often have looked at women—as sex objects. Thus the gay male reminds me of the guilt I deserve for making objects of other persons. He arouses my fear that now the tables might be turned. I, too, can be seen as just "a piece of meat." I can be womanized. Yet confusingly and at the same time, the gay male arouses another envy in me. He symbolizes the emotional vulnerability and intimate friendship that men might have with other men, relations that have been largely denied to me because of my homophobic fears.

In addition, we have learned to fear our own mortality. In spite of our religious proclamations, we so often live in dread of death and find our greatest reassurance in passing on life to our children. Instead of trusting resurrection, we trust procreation. Those who do not procreate represent the threat of death to everyone else. So the barren woman of biblical times was cursed, and in early New England she was persecuted as a witch. So also, homosexual people are seen as nonprocreative, reminding all of us of our dust factor. Today, with the current AIDS epidemic, they do so in a double way—they seem to be linked not only with nonprocreation but with an incurable, fatal disease. Then others of us must distance ourselves from and punish those who remind us too vividly that we, too, shall one day die.

Sexual stereotypes remind us that we all have a body. They remind us of what we have learned in bodily fears, envies, shame, and guilt. But if we do not know the gospel in our bodies, can we really know the gospel? When we lose the incarnational reality that God's embodiment continues in us all, we also lose our capacities for passion and caring, our hunger for justice. Homophobia and AIDS are particularly vivid reminders of what is true more broadly. When bodies are not holy, then neither are hungry children in our own towns; neither is flesh torn by torture in Latin America or by apartheid's guns in South Africa. How can I care for that flesh if I do not feel my own? Moral compassion is rooted in the life of the body.

## The Capacity for Connecting

Moral understanding is significantly of the body. So also is compassion. Finally, consider the bodily dimensions of our

capacity for connecting. The dualism that body ethics challenges here is the assumption that separation is more real
than connection—whether the separation is between spirit
and body in the self, the split between the self and the other,
or the gulf between the divine and the human. The problem
is the loss of a deep sense of communion, of relatedness. In
one way or another it is one of the fundamental issues that
pastoral counselors face daily with those they counsel.

In his well-known book *I and Thou*, Martin Buber said it
simply: "In the beginning is the relation."[7] Not one, not I,
not you, not even God, but the relation. "In the beginning is
the relation"—a deceptively simple yet radical statement for
the ears of anyone in a dualistic culture, particularly to those
of us reared on the individualism exemplified by the Lone
Ranger. I am increasingly persuaded that the anti-body tradition in the Christian West is the basic cause of our blindness
to life as fundamentally relational.

But if we know anything at all, it is in relation to our bodily
space. We use prepositions: in, over, under, between, beyond, beside, within. Each preposition depends upon an
instinctive sense of our own bodily location in relation to the
rest of the world. As children we learn (until we are taught
otherwise) that the fundamental reality with which we deal in
life is not disconnected objects or beings but relationships.

Long before we can understand any of this we must literally
be loved into being as human. We must be given the human
gift of the capacity to relate by being tenderly held, sensu-
ously nurtured by the parental body, talked into our own
speech, communicated into our own possiblities of communion. Pastoral counselors all too frequently see ways in which
the deprivation of this life-giving nurture has been devastating to the person deprived.

Socrates advised, "Know thyself." Surely counselors have
taken him seriously both in regard to themselves and as goals
of their clients' therapy. But I know myself only as I know the
profound relationality of my existence, the relationships that

bring health, those that bring disease, those that can be transformed.

To know myself as profoundly relational is to know myself as body. All of our relationships are mediated through our bodies, for it is in our embodiedness that we have our perception. It is in our emotions that we interact with the world. It is through our senses that we experience what it means to be a self in relation. It is our sexual, sensuous selves that ground our relatedness, and it is our sense of bodily integrity that grounds our power and capacity for vulnerability with others. And when there is bodily repression, when the body is deeply alienated, dis-eased, we lose our sense of connectedness to each other, to nature, yes, to the cosmos and to God.[8]

I am convinced that connectedness constitutes a particular problem and challenge for men. Whether male or female, we came into the world faced with two basic tasks of self-discovery. One is gender identity: who am I as male or female? The other is individuation: who am I as someone unique, unlike any other? In the crucial time of infancy and early childhood, virtually all of us were primarily nurtured by women, our mothers. This meant that we resolved those two early tasks of self-knowledge differently, depending on whether we were male or female. Girls experience themselves as being like their mothers, and gender identity seems to come naturally through the flow of that connection. Individuation is the problem. In contrast, to define themselves as male and masculine, boys must physically separate themselves from their mothers. Gender identity comes less easily and more painfully, and it comes precisely through individuation and pushing away. We who are male become skilled early in the arts of separation and, indeed, learn a painful lesson that stays with us a lifetime: connectedness, the erotic bonding with the most real person in our lives, is a threat to our masculinity. Eros is a threat to manhood.

The dynamics of separation play themselves out in the boy's

frustrated search for his father. Searching for positive clues to male identity, he discovers that his father (if, indeed, his is a two-parent family) is more physically and emotionally distant than his mother. And father's spoken messages about manhood are also counsels of separation: be your own man, keep your guard up. The mother's world is the soft, moist, timeless world of the body, the world of holding and caring. The father's world is prestige, power, and control, to be sure, but it is also distance, performance demands, and separation. The boy's boundaries not only have separated him from the intimate connection with others but also have minimized his connection to his body and inner emotional life.

And they have affected his relation to God—to God in male-constructed theologies and pieties wherein divinity is located in the distant, autonomous, wholly other, transcendent, omnipotent Sovereign. The message is clear: what is real in life is not connection but separation. When connection occasionally happens, it is wonderful, even miraculous, but separation is reality.

Near the end of Arthur Miller's *Death of a Salesman*, Biff, who has become a young man, desperately searches for connection with his father. Now taller than Willy, at one point Biff tearfully leans down and hugs him. But Willy sits there unmoving, uncomprehending, shrugging his shoulders at his wife on whom he has always depended to interpret his feelings. He doesn't hug his son back. Several years ago I saw Dustin Hoffman playing Willy Loman on Broadway. Before seeing the play I had read *The New Yorker* review, in which the only complaint about this superb production was that it was hard to hear some of the lines from the stage near the end because in the audience there were so many muffled sobs and so many noses being blown. It was true the night I was there, and mine were among them. The play's end brings no healing between father and son. The words at Willy's death are simple and stark: "He never knew who he was."

In my church in Minneapolis there is one stained-glass

window that particularly draws my attention Sunday mornings. It depicts the parable in which the forgiving father is embracing the prodigal son. Sometimes I find myself seeing in the window a forgiving son embracing a prodigal father. Sometimes I am not sure who the prodigal is or where the lines of divinity and humanity are. But some things are clear to me in those musings. It is clear to me that grace is real. That connection is what life is all about. And that gracious connection is a bodily reality.

To anyone committed to an incarnational faith, the grounding of our connectedness in the body should be no surprise—until we recognize how seldom we take incarnation, God's continuing embodiment, seriously. But what if, just what if, our very bodies themselves are God's revelations of the interrelatedness of all with all? Pierre Teilhard de Chardin put it memorably:

> The prevailing view has been that the body . . . is a *fragment* of the Universe, a piece completely detached from the rest and handed over to a spirit that informs it. In the future we shall have to say that the Body is the very Universality of all things. . . . *My* matter is not a *part* of the Universe that I possess *totaliter*: it is the *totality* of the Universe possessed by me *partialiter*.[9]

Differing religious traditions symbolize incarnationalism differently. We who are Christian name the Christ. Unfortunately, our Christologies often point more to disconnection than connection. Under the impact of a dualistic Greek metaphysics, the church's Christology became largely an abstract doctrine about the singular divinity of one figure named Jesus. He became understood as the unique and only genuine place of the joining of the divine and the human. The result was to confine the Christic reality to that one person and to deny it to everyone else. But as I understand Jesus, it was not his intent to control or to monopolize the

Christ presence but precisely the opposite: to share that reality with all who would respond.

In the orthodox view of Jesus as Christ, what was so often lost was the understanding that incarnation is the invitation to everyone. What was substituted was the belief in an unchanging God of perfection, whose divine love was utterly different from human love, whose divine body was utterly different from human bodies. Lost was the compelling experience of divine incarnation as the meaning and reality and life-giving power of every authentic relationship.

But what if we recover the conviction that the Christic reality is a possibility for all of us? Then we might have to take with some seriousness Luther's statement about being "Christ to the neighbor." And at least as frequently and of more importance, we might recognize the neighbor being Christ to us.

There will be times when we sense that somehow we are the embodiment of healing, power, and connection for another. When it happens we can only give thanks. When that occurs, we know in our better moments that we are not the *source* of that connecting power. The source is God. But we have been in that moment the necessary *meeting place* of God and human flesh, the crucial, even if fragmentary, embodiment of God.

And at least as frequently, there will be times when the person being counseled, the parishioner, the client, the patient, is Christ to us. It is the phenomenon in Matthew 25:37, 44, "Lord, when did we see you hungry, thirsty, a stranger, naked, sick, in prison?" Here is the stunning reversal. Christ is in "the wrong place!" Now we are not the Christlike counselors armed with strength, techniques, and professional skills to cure. Now it is the crucified one who is in the ditch, in the hospital bed, in the client's chair. Now it is the one reminding us of God's absence who paradoxically mediates God's presence. Now it is he or she who mediates God's vulnerability and weakness, thereby eliciting our own, and in our mutual need we are for the moment bonded with life-giving communion. It is still the Christic experience. It is still the embodied God. It is still the meeting with the cosmic love in and through human flesh. The Word still becomes flesh and dwells among us.

When this happens, Christ is present, often in the unlikely and in the unexpected. A few months before my friend Bill died, he and Bob telephoned us one Sunday afternoon. My wife's eighty-year-old mother was with us. Having spent a lifetime in a small town in South Dakota, she had never knowingly even met a gay man. Bob and Bill were calling to say that they would like to drop in with some bran muffins and brownies they had just baked. We told Mom they were coming. She had known from previous conversations about these friends that they were gay. Before they arrived, I told her, in addition, that they both had AIDS and that Bill didn't have much longer to live.

My wife and I were not sure what Mom's reaction would be. Wise and caring in so many ways, yet her long years had not prepared her for this encounter. What were her fears?

They came, and we visited for an hour or so. Soon after they left, we three sat down for a light Sunday evening supper. Their gifts of food were on the table along with a few other things. We did not know what Mom would eat. The conversation centered around their visit. She wanted to know more about these men, and finally she said, "I'm really glad I was here to meet your friends." And then, rather deliberately, "I believe I'll have one of those bran muffins." She ate two, and topped it off with a brownie, as did each of us. And never before has the sacrament been more real to me: the broken bread coming from Christ's broken bodies and giving life. And never before in my experience had the holy sacrament included brownies.

## CHAPTER 4

# Giving Care Through Counseling

## Liston O. Mills

A NUMBER OF QUESTIONS EMERGE WHEN ONE CONSIDERS the relation of care and counseling. Since it is usually assumed that counseling is a, perhaps the, primary mode of pastoral care, why should there be need of comment at all? Have the two become separated so that their relation is no longer obvious? Have the words care and counseling become so ambiguous that their meanings are no longer clear and the question of their relation reflects pastors' uncertainty about their purpose and function? Finally, does it matter that the words care and counseling are usually modified by the adjective pastoral? Does the pastor's concern with the cure-of-souls tradition affect pastoral understanding of care and counseling?

One thing is clear. An inquiry about caring through counseling assumes that counseling is an expression of caring. It becomes quite important, then, to understand the content of that care and to acknowledge the various influences on a definition of the term. For that reason I shall try to define

**Liston O. Mills**, Ph.D., is Oberlin Alumni Professor of Pastoral Theology and Counseling at the Divinity School, Vanderbilt University, Nashville.

"care" and to comment on "pastoral" care. Then I will cite several examples of the relation of care and counseling as they concern the cure of souls. Finally I shall ask how the relation between the two became problematic and offer possibilities for a revitalized understanding of them.

## Definitions

Efforts to determine the meaning of "care" are frustrated by the discovery that it has all but become a nonword. Its use in ordinary discourse may not refer to anything specific, and its use in pastoral-care circles may be influenced by anyone from William Glasser to Karl Barth. A survey of its etymology, however, reveals that care has to do with trouble and grief. It has to do with suffering, with a burdened state of mind, which may arise from fear or doubt or concern. Care also has to do with solicitude and with anxiety; it is the anxiety one experiences when one is charged to oversee and protect so as to preserve and guide. This latter meaning derives from the Latin *curare* and refers to taking care of, caring for, or having regard for. In this sense care indicates efforts to heal or to restore, to remedy or to preserve. Thus care has two dimensions. It may reflect the subjective experience of being troubled or grieved, such as a person who is "burdened with care." It may also refer to the attitude of solicitude, concern, and carefulness desirable in persons responsible for taking care of others.

Since pastoral care is located within the cure-of-souls tradition, the "soul" is the object of this solicitude. John McNeill described the soul as the essence of human personality and the seat of a person's relatedness to God.[1] The soul, then, is related to the body, but it is not a mere function of bodily life. It is capable of extensive ranges of experience and susceptible to disorder and anguish, while at the same time it is endowed with possibilities of blessedness within and beyond the order of time. McNeill goes on to describe the cure of souls as the sustaining and curative treatment of persons in matters that reach beyond the requirements of bodily life.

In the history of the church, pastoral care may be understood in both a broad and a narrow sense. Broadly seeking, pastoral care may refer to any pastoral act motivated by a sincere devotion to the well-being of another. Thus liturgical forms and ritual acts may reflect care just as education and social action may. Narrowly speaking, pastoral care refers to the more intensive dimension of the larger tasks of ministry, such as conversations with persons or groups who seek interpersonal, moral, or spiritual guidance. Traditionally such conversations were discussed under the rubrics of admonition, edification, consolation, and sometimes discipline. More recently, in the mid-twentieth century, Seward Hiltner and William Clebsch and Charles Jaekle suggested that care includes the pastoral functions of healing, sustaining, guiding, and reconciling.[2] Clebsch and Jaekle also insist that the care must involve matters of "ultimate concern," that is, the troubles must foster a deeper faith in and relation to God. Thus they place themselves squarely within the cure-of-souls tradition.

It becomes obvious in any survey of the history of pastoral care that there are diverse understandings of its content. It is also clear that what constitutes pastoral care in any given era is rooted in the basic religious convictions of the community. To be sure, care is also rooted in the differing historical, political, and social fabric of particular communities. But at its base, matters of Christology, soteriology, and ecclesiology cannot be set aside if as ministers we are to understand what pastoral care means, if we are to sense our obligation to one another, and if we are to determine to some degree what constitutes "helping." Clarity about the meaning of care determines its relation to counseling.

## Examples of Historical Care and Counseling

Examples from the history of pastoral care demonstrate that its definition depended on a way of understanding relatedness to God, and its ingredients were judged according to whether they enhanced or detracted from that relatedness. In other words, care did not consist of indiscriminate good deeds, however well-intentioned. Instead it was an expression of fundamental theological understandings, which were made manifest in counseling.

Certainly the best-known example of the relation of care and counseling among the church fathers is Pope Gregory the Great. His *Pastoral Rule* was written in the sixth century at a time of social and political turmoil, a time during which monasteries and clergy became the primary vehicles for the transmission of order in an unruly society. By describing the priest as the governor of souls, Gregory sought to codify and pass on the wisdom of the church regarding clergy responsibilities in pastoral care. Order was maintained by guiding troubled souls into faith and moral uprightness. Thus he encouraged the distraught to bring their distress to the church so that its priests, as physicians of the soul, might "meet moral diseases" with compassion. Gregory's powers of discernment led him to assume that care provided in depth would invariably involve deeper spiritual issues. He was an astute observer of human nature, who developed a typology of personality—for example, the simple, the insincere, the bashful, the impudent—and enumerated the particular temptations likely to characterize each type. Later he delineated different approaches, or "treatments," for the various sins. Always his counsel had as its intent strengthening the parishioner's soul; the care was crucial; it involved salvation and eternity.

The relation of care and counseling implicit in Gregory's

concept is also evident in Luther and in Roman Catholic writers after the Council of Trent. For Luther "spiritual counsel is always concerned above all else with faith—nurturing, strengthening, establishing, practicing, faith."[3] The attention devoted to casuistry and to spiritual direction after 1550 in the Roman Catholic Church shows a similar concern. Questions of conscience became primary among Jesuit and later, Redemptorist priests. Spiritual directors such as St. Francis de Sales, St. Vincent de Paul, and Bishop F. de S. de La M. Fénelon provide a rich treasure of literature on their efforts to inspire a higher level of spiritual life.

One final example of the relation of counseling to care may be found in the Puritans, especially the English scholar Richard Baxter.[4] Care to Baxter meant that he spent fifteen to sixteen hours each week visiting in people's homes to instruct them in the faith, "searching men's hearts and setting home the saving truths." Pastoral visitation also involved visiting the sick, "helping them prepare for a fruitful life or a happy death." But care involved private counseling as well. William Perkins, the Puritan divine, said, "As the lawyer is [a counselor] for their estates and the physician for their bodies," so the minister is the "counselor for their souls," who "must be ready to give advice to those that come to him with cases of conscience."[5]

Baxter defined his care as consisting of two things. First, it had to reveal to persons that happiness or good which must be their ultimate end. Second, it had to introduce them to the right means to attain that end, helping them to utilize those means and interfering with any contrary efforts. It was clear to Baxter that unskilled counselors might aggravate situations, so he urged pastors to "have a care to qualify themselves." Any number of Puritan manuals provided instruction on dealing with all manner of questions of conscience, especially with acute anxiety and despair. A good counselor, it was said, would bear with "peevishness" and with "disordered and distempered affections and actions." He would share sorrows and tears, listen well, guard secrets, and not be censorious where consciences were "unduly disturbed." Baxter emphasized the importance of such ministries by arguing that the pastoral office was much more than "those men have taken it to be, who think it consists in preaching and administering the sacraments only."

In summary, pastoral care traditionally reflected a theological diagnosis of human distress, which then was specifically expressed in counseling. Different expressions of pastoral care manifest different understandings of both the distress and its remedy. But each expression perceived relatedness to God, however described, as the human beatitude, and the intent of a pastor's care and counseling was to address the soul's anguish in its separation from God.

## The Modern Separation of Care and Counseling

What has been said up to now was generally true of the relation between care and counseling through the nineteenth century. To understand how the relation between the two became tenuous, it is necessary to understand the effect on them of the rise of industrial technology and the shift in cultural values in the late nineteenth and early twentieth centuries, and the emergence of alternative understandings of care.

Obviously there have always been understandings of the soul's distress and of its care that were different from those of the church. Beginning with the Enlightenment, however, these alternatives became more persuasive, and attention shifted from theological concerns to a preoccupation with human beings as the measure of things. These new perceptions reached a high point in the nineteenth century and found expression in the work of Darwin, Marx, the anthropologists Emil Durkheim and Bronislaw Malinowski, and, especially for this discussion, Freud. Philip Rieff describes this shift as a cultural "deconversion" and "reconversion."[6] The deconversion was the dissolution of the unitary system of common beliefs and symbols of the Judeo-Christian tradition. The reconversion was to belief in science, and it was expressed in an anti-creedal, analytic attitude that promised to teach us the truth about ourselves and our world without recourse to theology or metaphysics.

For the purposes of this discussion it is important to acknowledge that the demise of these cultural myths, collective ideologies, and communal affirmations of faith profoundly affected Western society's understanding of itself and of pastoral care and counseling. Don Browning notes that work in the psychological sciences, as for example in Freud and Carl Rogers, provided theories of the person that considered moral expectations to be at the root of much neurotic dysfunction.[7] In dealing with human distress and its alleviation in therapy, these psychologists sought a stance free of religious values, which called theological understandings into question. The caring professions, such as religion, psychology, and medicine, became increasingly specialized and separate from one another. Each of these professions developed distinct institutional traditions and sought in relatively autonomous ways to help those suffering spiritual, psychological, or physical difficulties.

I trust that I am not minimizing the substantial gains represented by the efforts of the psychological scientists. What I have intended is to provide a context for understanding the strain within the religious community between pastoral care and counseling and their theological mooring. It should come as no surprise that academics and pastors who were sensitive to human pain found that the developments in psychology and psychotherapy provided a promising and refreshing resource for their work. For they, too, understood that moralism and legalism defeated care, and they were aware that vital faith was elusive within the confines of the propositional theology many had learned. For a host of persons, the psychological sciences seemed to offer fresh understandings of human being and precise, realistic modes of care and counseling.

In the mid-1950s H. Richard Niebuhr reported that the focusing of attention on pastoral care was one of the most important developments in theological education. The immediate relevance of dynamic theory for pastoral work made the psychological sciences seem important for intense study and led to the appointment of faculty and the establishment of required courses in the area. Yet these advances were not without costs. One cost was that the excitement generated by the new approaches caused many to neglect their theological heritage; the subject matter of pastoral care was increasingly funded and maintained by its relation to the psychological discipline rather than by the theological discipline. A second cost was the growing separation of care and counseling. Care became a general activity, whereas counseling became a specialty. Thus care was part of the communal life, meanings, and traditions of the church, whereas counseling lost its specifically theological character and intent.

It would be a mistake to place the entire responsibility for these developments on the shoulders of those committed to giving pastoral care. As Edward Farley suggests, confusion surrounded theology itself.[8] Farley explains that the development of theology as a specialized discipline fostered its separation from the practical dimensions of ministry. He, along with David Tracy, Thomas Ogletree, and Don Browning, encouraged conversation on just this issue. It is important to observe here that although pastoral care was being criticized for its dependence on the psychological sciences, few theologians showed interest or offered support in dealing with the pressing issues pastoral care raised. Theirs was a different agenda.

One additional contribution to the separation of care and counseling reflects the general shift in values in North Amer-

ican culture. Robert Bellah in *Habits of the Heart* describes
this as a shift in mores, that is, in the notions, opinions, and
ideas that shape our mental habits and routine practices.[9] The
rise of technology, for example, is frequently cited as an
occasion for a fundamental redefinition of human life whereby
a sense of contingency is replaced by an illusion of control.
Society's scientific and technological successes lead us to
conclude that our lives—work, family, leisure—should function as efficiently as our machines. If they do not, we assume
that something can be done, for our confidence in science is
complete. Nowhere is this effort to "legislate the grotesque
out of life" more apparent than in our attitude to health. It
has become a primary value, so that whether one eats yogurt,
jogs, plays the guitar, or practices yoga—all is in the name of
health. This subtle expectation that we alone are totally
responsible and should be in control of ourselves and the
events and persons around us creates immense frustration
when we are confronted with senseless suffering, recalcitrant
children, or unsolvable problems. It bespeaks a loss of tran-
scendence and the participation in an order of reality where
incompleteness and failure can be expected and are not
occasions for despair.

   Alongside the obligation to control our lives is the value of
individual fulfillment, which has displaced communal obligation. Bellah argues that the most distinctive feature of twen-
tieth-century North American society is the division of life
into functional compartments: home and workplace, work and
leisure, public and private. The tracks to success in the world
of work are laid out by government and schools, business
corporations and the professions; the individual's task is to
balance these competing claims. The function of domesticity
is to provide the love and intimacy that will insulate people
from, or enable them to endure, the competitive pressures of
work.

   Bellah argues that the manager and the therapist are the
crucial characters in the move to personal fulfillment. Success
at work, under the direction of the manager, leads to in-

creased income, status, and authority, which are the sources of freedom. The therapist focuses on the individual, helping him or her to choose the roles and commitments that will ensure satisfaction and effectiveness in life. What in earlier times were understood as normative commitments or moral imperatives become in this framework alternative strategies to self-fulfillment. Communal values and obligations are lost amidst the competing understandings of who we are and what we need. The effect of this quest for fulfillment, these mores that guide our decisions and behaviors, is to encourage us to think of all commitments in terms of our needs and well-being. Marriage, work, politics, and religious involvement are all paths to the enhancement of our sense of individual well-being.

What I have described as an ingredient to the separation of care and counseling certainly alters our definition of each. For their definition as theological constructs, as given by Baxter or Gregory, intended to enrich or encourage our relatedness to God within the religious community, is clouded by mores and values that redefine them as sociocultural and psychological constructs with the goal of individual fulfillment. Moreover, counseling as a specialty probably participates more completely in this separation than does general pastoral care within congregations. But each is influenced in fundamental ways by the culture and by psychological theory, and each seeks ways to renew or reintroduce a theological dimension to giving care and counseling. Put another way, the question of relatedness to God as an essential ingredient in care and counseling is again being raised.

## Present-day Understandings of Care and Counseling

In the late twentieth century many people in the field of pastoral care have begun to give attention to the dilemmas I describe. Indeed as long ago as the 1950s an article appeared in the *Journal of Pastoral Care* entitled "The Babylonian Captivity of Pastoral Care," which described pastors' dependence on psychology to the neglect of their heritage. Along the way Wayne Oates, Seward Hiltner, William Oglesby, and a host of others have sought to address these issues. More recently professionals in the field, including the late Paul Pruyser, Charles Gerkin, John Patton, and Don Browning, seem to be more interested in the theological integrity of counseling than in proliferation of counseling centers.

Experiences in the field have dictated this attention to the theological contours of pastoral care and counseling. Consider, for example, Carl Rogers. Rogers had absolute confidence in the scientific method. He also had absolute confidence in human beings, a confidence that may have been misplaced. He thought that since science shows us how things work, it could also show us how *we* work, with the hope that, knowing the cause of all things, we would be able to control all things.

Psychology and psychotherapy, then, and in this case Rogers, wanted to show us why we felt bad, why we felt unhappy, inadequate, and inferior, on the assumption that if we knew the reasons, if we knew, after all, that this is the way we are in the evolutionary scheme of things, we would stop scolding ourselves, accept ourselves, and find peace and fulfillment. But Ernest Becker reminds us that science as represented by psychology can only find part of the reason for our experience, "the part caused by objects, trying to be good for them, fearing them, fearing leaving them, and the like."[10] We should not minimize the importance of this partial discovery. Persons freed from neurotic guilt, the unnecessary conflicts of the past, the ways in which they are chained and blocked from development, do indeed become more honest with themselves, more sure of themselves, and enjoy more freedom and spontaneity in their lives and relations.

But Rogers erred when he identified the guilt and unhappiness growing out of past relations with persons and institutions as *the* human problem. Actually it is only *part* of the problem. When the distraught emerge from the consulting room or the encounter group, there looms before them still the problem of why they are alive, why they have problems, experience terror, are mortal. All the therapy available does not finally tell us who we are and why we must die and what we must do to make our life a triumph.

It is not that persons in pastoral care have become disenchanted with psychology but that human experience has summoned us to a different view of life. For we have learned that simply to be human is to confess that something is wrong. To be human is to be aware of a rift so deep in our lives that we frequently can only use the language of tragedy. And the question of how this tragedy is to be understood and at least in part overcome is the central theme of both theology and the helping professions. Pastoral care is rooted in this fundamental human problem, as is all serious theology. It is rooted in this sense of incompleteness and powerlessness, in the confession that something is wrong, and in this quest for the gift of life itself.

This understanding of the human dilemma implies that our lives are reflections of our efforts to come to terms with our alienation and powerlessness. Human life is by definition a quest for grace. Pastoral care and its expression in counseling is a response to this quest. The psychologist Karen Horney reminds us that much of our care comes in general terms. It consists of the gifts we offer and receive in daily interchange. It is the manner in which we support and sustain each other, the friendships, smiles, and solicitude that come each day and that, though often unacknowledged, literally keep us alive. Counseling is a specific and particular instance of that care. It is the quest for grace linked with another person's care, which is that person's willingness to participate in that quest.

Obviously when I speak in terms of the rift in life and the

fragility of it I have gone against those individualists who understand beatitude to rest in achievement, advancement, and accumulation. For I have pointed to the essential vulnerability of human life, and if I am in any sense correct, then the question is more fundamental than any theory of therapy will answer. The question becomes, How can I be strong, how can I grow, how can I flourish in a world that seems bent on my undoing? The question does not have to do with the description and management of life; it has instead to do with the gift of life itself.

Pastoral counseling as care becomes an invitation to relationship and to community. But it is a particular sort of community, one that understands itself as depending constantly on the gift of life in grace. Thus it invites us, first, to acknowledge the truth of our lives. I have always been taught that to diagnose is to grasp things as they are so that one will be able to do the right thing. To grasp things as they are is to admit human incompleteness and our neurotic attempts to seal ourselves off from that knowledge by bravado and pretense. Symptom, in other words, is not simply pathology. It is also a way to avoid what we fear to be the truth about ourselves. By encouraging us to engage in what we think to be true, pastoral counseling as care invites us to discover another and deeper truth.

Again, pastoral counseling as care invites us to participate in a relationship and community in which it is safe to be both autonomous and dependent. The opportunity to acknowledge the truth implies that those with whom one shares this truth will not exploit it. It offers the prospect of learning to trust again, and this, in turn, means that persons can admit their need for and indebtedness to one another. The fact that there are no strings attached means that such a relation encourages the self to be itself, to come to itself, and to revel in its uniqueness. Recently I spoke with a woman who for a variety of medical and developmental reasons has not been able to lay hold of her considerable gifts. She appears on the threshold of affirming herself and I was somewhat inappropriately encouraging her, when she paused and said to me: "Liston, you don't understand. All my life I have been told that I could not be what I glimpse now I may become." She was right. I didn't understand. But the invitation to relationship gave her the opportunity to explore the possibility and to catch this glimpse. It comforted her, if comfort is taken to mean giving encouragement and lending one's heart to someone.

Such care in pastoral counseling enables persons to evaluate or come to terms with their place in life and the world. One's place is ordinarily defined in terms of externals. It stems from whom we know or the clothes we wear or the schools we attended. We are put in our place when others learn where we live and hear us speak. Pastoral counseling as care is an invitation to discover a new basis for self and worth. Such an invitation is endemic to Christian faith. Symbols such as the image of God, the children of God, and the people of God all point to fundamental truths about our identity as persons. They tell us of our worth and value and cause us to treasure what we are rather than rely on the assessments of strangers.

In the crucible of pastoral counseling as care, persons are given the opportunity to discover what they believe. Paul Pruyser mentioned how strange it is that people do not acknowledge their most deeply held convictions until old age; only then do they begin to share those values that have sustained and guided them throughout their lives. I suspect that one reason for this delay is that many of us are confused about what we do believe. In relation and community we not only discover what is true and valuable for us, we also have opportunity to test it with others. Moreover, the experience of relation and community makes it possible for some of us to believe. One comes to belief and trust in relation, or at least one comes to times when it is possible to believe and trust.

Pastoral counseling as care is also an occasion to accept judgment. For years we have held that acceptance, which we equate with grace, and judgment are two different things.

Actually judgment is endemic to acceptance. Acceptance makes judgment both inevitable and bearable. Martin Luther said that the depth of one's experience of grace was directly proportional to one's experience of sin. And in Christian faith the meaning of the cross has always involved these two messages. This central symbol of the faith reflects the alienation of persons from what is central and essential in life, while at the same time it holds before us the promise of renewal and restoration. Pastoral counseling invites one to deal with what one knows oneself to be and not have it become one's undoing.

One final dimension of pastoral counseling as care involves coming to community and admitting our need for a wisdom greater than our own. One of the mistaken notions of young counselors is that they should always understand and know what is happening in their interchanges with others. Eventually as counselors we discover that such is not the case, that not only do we not know but in many instances we cannot know. This frustration is often present when persons ask us what they should do. The simple truth is that usually we do not know. However, as part of a community with a heritage and a communal wisdom I as counselor can participate in an exploration of those things of which I am unsure. To be related to such a community is to have a sense of boundary, of direction, and of steadfastness. As counselors we can "reason together" as we seek to discern our way, and we can call upon the wisdom of those who have gone before and who also have sought their way. We can do it in the company of those who, like us, were destined and committed to the task of discerning grace, the gift of life.

To conclude with a traditional term, pastoral counseling as care offers blessing. To come to relation with others, to the truth about ourselves, to a sense of place and worth, to know judgment undergirded with grace, and to discover a community in which the individual may ponder questions with others is blessing. Such community fosters hope, and hope, it is said, does not disappoint us. The rift no longer determines our lives. Yet not everyone responds to this counsel; some walk away. But even then it is important for the counselor to see that there is no contradiction, no fundamental distinction, between the intent of the ministry of the church in giving pastoral care and the final intent of counseling.

Several years ago a former student of mine wrote to share a quotation he had discovered. In his letter he said that the lines from Aeschylus were something I would like "because it has finally occurred to me that this is what you were trying to teach me." He cited the lines:

> In our sleep pain which cannot forget, falls
> drop by drop upon our hearts, until, in our
> despair, against our will, comes wisdom
> through the awful grace of God.

Pastoral counseling as care is simply a special instance in which to invite participation in the pain so that we may know that awful grace of God.

## CHAPTER 5

# Intimacy and Relationships in Counseling

## Sidney Callahan

THE INTIMACY OF THE COUNSELING RELATIONSHIP PRO-
duces a particular set of challenging ethical questions. These
questions become more complicated when the counselor is a
religious believer who is engaged in a pastoral or care-giving
role. My contention is that the intimate relationships of
counseling are different from other professional and personal
relationships; indeed, this special intimacy is integral to the
success of the whole counseling enterprise. When one understands the force of this peculiar intimacy, certain ethical
dilemmas that emerge become more clearly understandable,
if not more easily resolved.

### Intimacy and the Nature of Counseling

Certain observers might distinguish different types of counseling from psychotherapy or see pastoral counseling as differ-

Sidney Callahan, Ph.D., D.Litt., teaches psychology at Mercy College,
Dobbs Ferry, New York.

ent from other kinds of counseling, but I see all of these helping activities as bearing too close a family resemblance to one another to categorize them separately. All face-to-face counseling is a form of focused, structured, person-to-person dialogue and deliberation whose goal is to help another. Even though psychiatrists may define themselves as members of the medical profession, physicians who diagnose disease and prescribe drugs for a person's mental illness, some form of face-to-face counseling must be involved. For psychologists, social workers, counselors, pastors, or nonprofessionals who become engaged in structured, interpersonal helping relationships, the presence or absence of professional labels or the exchange of money does little to change the reality of what goes on.

The person-to-person relationships in counseling and psychotherapy are intimate, but the intimacy differs in kind from the forms of intimacy experienced in marriage, friendship, and family relationships. Counseling usually is initiated by some crisis or at least by some serious doubt, upheaval, or felt need, which is precipitating some decision or change in a person's life. One person's need for counseling initiates the special, intimate relationship. The person in need of help opens his or her inner consciousness to the counselor. This intimacy may be similar to the way one talks with a spouse, family member, or close friend; but since the counseling relationship is usually time structured, short-term, unilateral, and confidential, the intimacy is unique.

Ironically, the psychological, intimate disclosures of self in counseling can be more profound than those in committed, long-term relationships. One can be more secure and safe and less inhibited when one need not worry about hurting, betraying, or alarming others by one's openness in recounting and analyzing the inner self's flow of consciousness or in giving accounts of personal behavior. The counselor, as a person sought out in special circumstances, is not a part of one's everyday, ongoing social interactions; the counselor, qua counselor, does not aim to be a permanent life partner of those he or she counsels, with corresponding reciprocal obligations and expectations.

Prior commitments in the rest of life before a person seeks counseling shape and may inhibit other ongoing dialogues and communication opportunities. The counseling relationship is set apart, private, special, and unilateral; it is therefore more detached and potentially freer from ordinary constraints. The confidentiality assumed in counseling comes from its special, set-apart intimacy. A patient visiting a physician may undress in order to have his or her body examined; in counseling, a person is made vulnerable by self-revelation and examination in depth of inner consciousness.

The quality of the intimacy is crucial to the success of the counseling enterprise. Other roles in life, such as those of employee, citizen, student, or teacher, can be successfully filled without psychological intimacy. By contrast, the need for positive, emotionally open communication in counseling has been recognized as necessary by theorists trying to explain why counseling works to help people change and heal their lives.[1]

The positive effects of counseling or psychotherapeutic encounters have been established in research,[2] but the explanations of how they work have been debated. Change in a person can be described as a process of unfreezing, reeducation, and refreezing[3]. Change emerges when a person unfreezes by learning to feel new emotions, think new thoughts, and engage in new behaviors. The interpersonal experiences of the counseling relationship may bring about change when there are new patterns in self-to-self interactions and self-to-other relationships accompanying new behaviors in the environment.[4] All these forms of change are interrelated when a person is helped by counseling.

Counseling is never simply the transmission of new information and directives; one cannot counsel effectively by telegram. Complicated human organisms only receive and fully process those messages that engage their personal attention. Our emotional personal responses to the communicator or source of the message allow us to pay attention and hear the message; we receive new information from those persons to whom we feel emotionally attuned. The medium is the message when it comes to interpersonal communication.

Some of the most interesting new work on the development of the sense of self emphasizes the importance from infancy of our human abilities to share emotional subjective states with another self without language.[5] As with mother and child, two people can pay attention to the same thing, cooperate in a task, and share emotional reactions without language. The extensive research on nonverbal channels of communication makes clear that face, eyes, voice, posture, use of space, and gesture contribute to human communication of feelings and meanings. Now we can begin to understand scientifically the power of mime and the effective acting in silent movies.

This emotional, intersubjective, person-to-person sharing, or mutual attunement of feelings, is almost the definition of intimacy—words proffered by themselves do not do the job. A person can be speaking and giving verbal information that is supposedly self-disclosing but without providing congruent emotional messages in all the other channels we can use to communicate with one another.[6] Pseudo-intimacy and pseudo-mutuality are discernible. The emphasis in counseling on elusive qualities such as warmth, empathy, authenticity, intuitive understanding, and trust points to the importance of the nonverbal dimensions of person-to-person relationships. If counselors cannot emotionally "connect" with those whom they counsel, they will fail, no matter what professional training they have had or what techniques they use. Some people have been found to have "therapeutic personalities," and what they do helps those they counsel to change and heal.[7]

Effective counseling gives hope and immediate comfort and support when, as usually happens, a person comes into counseling feeling demoralized and in need of help. The support given produces affective intimacy and empathy, which then allow the counselor to do some reeducation, to give some explanation or cognitive framework to what the person is experiencing. Once the emotional connection is made, once heart speaks to heart, then the power of reason, language, and explanation can be exerted to help a person to think more rationally and productively. Having some intellectual grasp of a situation and some new ways to make sense of things are steps in achieving a new ability to cope. The recent emergence of rational, cognitive therapies that focus on reeducating a troubled person's thinking has once again pointed to the effectiveness of reasoning together in counseling.[8]

New thoughts lead to new emotions, new images, and new plans for action. New behavior induces new emotions, new experiences, and new reflections. Education and personal change are always circular and interactive. The personal reeducation in counseling may be further strengthened if the counselor is taken as a model to be imitated. One therapeutic strength of all self-help movements depends on the direct learning available from peers modeling new ways to live. A counselor can also be a model as well as helping or guiding a person in trying new, more adaptive behaviors.

Refreezing is also important, as a counselor supports the stabilizing of new ways of life. The final goal of successful counseling and change is to create a situation where the counselor is no longer needed, and the person has learned to help himself or herself and cope in new ways without the counselor. Closure, separation, and termination are the final challenges in counseling relationships. Both parties have to be able to let go after the counseling process has been completed.

## General Ethical Issues in Counseling

Ethical issues in counseling relationships arise from the unusually intimate nature of counseling. The modern philosopher Stephen Toulmin has distinguished between an ethics of intimacy and an ethics of strangers.[9] He has maintained that in an ethics of strangers one resorts to universal principles and applies them impartially. But he also has seen that there is an ethics of discretion and intimacy, which can operate only among those who know each other well, as in the family or immediate local community. Those who coexist in intimate relationships can make specific case-by-case decisions relying on their shared values, experience, and special knowledge of particular circumstances.

The intimacy of the counseling relationship makes it one in which an ethics of intimacy and discretion will apply. But this useful distinction between what may be owed to strangers and what may be appropriate for intimate relationships needs more development in a larger, overall ethical framework. I hold that the ethics of intimacy must be grounded upon a prior commitment to a universal ethics of strangers. With intimates we may go beyond our universal principled obligations to strangers, but we may never fall below the acceptable standards applicable for any person we might encounter.

For instance, a man morally cannot assault his wife and children any more than he could if they were strangers, but he can be obligated to nurture and support them in more positive ways. With those with whom we are intimate, such as family and friends, we may be called to go the second mile and make greater efforts, with more investment of self or more sacrifices, than we would with strangers. Our special roles as intimates may also induce us to intrude and persist in certain efforts that we would not make with others; or sometimes as next of kin we may be called upon to make more fateful decisions for that person than we would for a stranger.

But an ethics of intimacy can never give us the right to do more harm to an intimate than to someone else.

Counseling can be included in the category of an ethics of intimacy and discretion. Counselors owe the basic universal obligations to those they try to help, but a counselor involved in an intimate counseling relationship may make specific decisions in individual cases, which are aimed at benefiting the other person. These ethical decisions of discretion can hardly be decided simply by adhering to universal principles embodied in the common legal and ethical policies set up by professional groups. An ethics of intimacy and discretion may impel a counselor to go beyond average expectable standards as he or she deals with the more subtle and personally challenging moral issues that emerge in the counseling relationship.

As for the basic foundational ethics of strangers in the counseling relationship, here the universal governing principles would be the obvious straightforward moral obligations to do no harm and to live according to acceptable public standards. Anyone who comes to any counselor should certainly be protected from deception, fraud, assault, sexual abuse, seduction, financial exploitation, the breaking of confidentiality, and incompetence arising from either a lack of training or impairment from drugs or illness. The traditional legal and ethical standards of anyone providing a service in a community or interacting with others in public relationships should apply in counseling.

Aside from evil intentions or severe impairments, there can exist more ambiguous moral problems in assessing a person's competence to do counseling. A recent directive to licensed psychologists from a professional state licensing body gave instructions on the ethical guidelines in force and then added the intriguing command, "Do not do anything you know you aren't competent to do." The problem, of course, is correctly assessing one's own competency. We are aware of the infamous case of a nearly blind surgeon claiming competence to operate, despite the fact that his patients died at an alarming rate. Counselors do not bury their mistakes; the suicides of those in treatment may often have been unavoidable no matter what measures were taken. Nor, despite the occasional malpractice suit for gross negligence, is there much reliable evidence from those counseled to provide responses about the quality of counselor competency.

In fact, when counseling goes well, the persons counseled can absorb their new experiences, achieve health, and proceed to forget the cooperative labor and struggle that went on. Client response, like that of students, is not always valid. Moreover, certain personality or temperamental or cognitive styles or ethnic matches between the counselor and persons who seek help can be more effective than others.[10] Just as certain people can more likely be friends, so certain matches in counseling are more successful. In such a subtle undertaking it is hard to measure competency and more difficult for the counselor to assess where he or she stands in the ranks of those with therapeutic personalities and gifts of healing.

The situation is made even more complex by the fact that some of the greatest counselors have been humbly in touch with their own ignorance and supremely conscious of their lack of knowledge. The mystery of the human heart is not easily fathomed or summed up by psychological theories or technological approaches. When it comes to character and personality change, scientific theories can only go so far. The counselor may not ever fully understand why certain persons decide to respond and change and others continue on self-destructive paths. (Various religious believers have been driven to theories of predestination or the effects of karma from past lives!) Psychological healing is in great part more determined by the self than imposed from outside. Counselors can talk of establishing a supportive or therapeutic alliance with the person who wishes to get well, but the language does not go far in explaining the forces of healing.[11] Good counselors often feel that what they are doing is at most acting as midwife at the birth of health or sometimes simply providing the occasion or excuse for the inner healing processes to occur.

Yet as in all intimate relationships, one can impede or harm others through ignorance, carelessness, weakness, or moral flaws. A counselor who is wise in the ways of self-deception in others should never abandon self-examination and self-criticism. There should be a strong moral commitment and desire to do well and serve competently. This goal can be met by seeking the advice and scrutiny of other people who do counseling. Continuing professional training can help, as well as group supervision or informal support networks. When warranted by consultation there will be occasions when counselors should withdraw and refer persons seeking help to a more appropriate source. Sometimes one can clearly know that one is not competent for a task.

Decisions about one's competence are primary examples of ethical decision making that combine the ethics of intimacy (with one's self) and the universal principles appropriate to all human beings. In reality, ethical decision making does not seem to be a linear, deductive process, which moves from axioms to conclusions. It is more of a fusion of personal and principled considerations and a recursive back-and-forth engagement. One oscillates between different levels and styles of thinking and personal emotional reactions to one's partial solutions. Moral deliberation is dynamic and multi-modal, as a person tries to come to a balanced solution in which all one's resources, reason, intuition, principles, and emotions are integrated. As more and more philosophers are now acknowledging, changing views of the facts and changes in feeling and action are interrelated in weighing moral arguments and moral decisions.[12]

For that matter, most of ethics is not concerned with big decisions but with the smaller decisions that daily shape character. Those matters that we attend to day by day go into our long-term memories and thereafter shape the mind, which meets and filters future consciousness. [13] Our personalities and moral character, our habits of the heart, arise from the incremental self-shaping engendered by the many small decisions of whom and what we choose to love and make the object of our effort and attention and where we shall do it. The good counselor gradually creates the self who can help others; the person who results will, or will not, be able to make wise ethical decisions employing sound principles and exercising wise discretion. The personal character is formed and then meets the new moral challenges that constantly emerge in the counseling relationship.

## Specific Moral Challenges in Counseling

Certain problems that arise from the intimacy of the counseling relationship will be familiar to anyone who engages in any practice consisting of personal interventions in other people's lives. The unknown effects of one's actions can never be fully predicted. A counselor is always dealing with uncertainty and risk in deciding what to do or say or how to intervene or interpret what is happening in the counseling session.

The interpersonal nature of counseling means that a counselor's intuitions about, and personal responses to, a person can be seen as signals of what is happening at deeper levels of consciousness. The counselor may think, "If this person affects me in this fashion, he may also come across this way to others." Or a person may appear angry or sad, while overtly denying it. But for a counselor to risk harm by making impulsive interpretations and interventions may be a mistake. Most counselors will, I think rightly, be quite cautious and test their intuitions a long while before using confrontation or an intrusive strategy that might be painful or provocative. Patience and delicacy are certainly called for in the beginning of a counseling relationship. The safest ethical course is to take only the most reasonable risks when dealing with another person who is in need of help and therefore vulnerable.

The same cautious stance can be the safest approach to innovative techniques sometimes used in counseling, such as hypnosis or role playing or paradoxical instructions. In my opinion, all strategies that rely on deception, i.e., they cannot be explained before they are applied, should be eschewed. People who come for counseling must be honestly and openly acquainted with what will take place so that they can give informed consent to the methods that will be used to help them. Informed consent is impossible if the counselor cannot tell people that the covert purpose of a paradoxical instruction is to make them feel or do the opposite thing from the overt command. Any therapeutic effects brought about by strategic tricks may be offset by the person's sense that he or she has been covertly manipulated. If, however, the counselor seeks cooperation or consent beforehand for hypnosis or role playing, explained and labeled as such, this strategic move may be ethical, so long as the counselor is competently trained and can protect the person seeking help from coming to any harm.

Most of the ethical problems in intimate counseling involve the problematic use of the power that the counselor possesses by virtue of the circumstances. Inevitably there is an inequality in power, because, if nothing else, the counselor has been sought out as a helper. The person who seeks is more in need and so more vulnerable. The universal tendency in such helping relationships is for the one seeking help to regress from adulthood and look upon the helper as if he or she were an idealized, nurturing parent. The seeker often regards the helper with belief in the helper's power and hope of a cure.

Thus some overestimation of the counselor may be productive at the beginning of counseling. But as the person being counseled becomes less needy of help, so he or she has less need to invest in any illusion of benevolent power on the part of any magic helper. The ability to see a counselor more realistically is a mark of the healing process. The wise counselor knows this will happen eventually but does not hurry the process when it would not benefit the person in need. In the most successful counseling, just as in successful parenting or teaching, power will gradually become more or less equalized. The good counselor, teacher, or parent is trying to work himself or herself out of a job and have the client, student, or child take over.

As long as the power differential lasts, however, and is exercised in a private setting, it is important that caution and restraint govern so that the power of intimacy is used and not abused. One question that then emerges for a religious or pastoral counselor is whether it is a use or abuse of power to engage in ethical confrontation or religious guidance while counseling a person. This crucial issue always appears in the ethics of counseling: how does the counselor deal with the challenge of conflicting ethical and religious standards?

## Ethical and Religious Conflict in Pastoral Counseling

The problem of ethical and religious conflict may not arise if a counselor has been chosen particularly because of holding beliefs similar to those of the person seeking help. If the help sought is overtly religious or moral counseling, openly offered under religious auspices, there is little difficulty. The helper has been asked to help because he or she will be able to integrate ethical and religious wisdom in the counseling. Sometimes the explicit focus of the counseling is spiritual growth and spiritual direction. Spiritual direction today is much the same as any other form of counseling, but the purpose is usually to further growth rather than to deal with particular problems. There is a need but not the same kind of need that a person suffering from grief or substance abuse, for example, presents. Tact, delicacy, wisdom, and skill are still necessary in these intimate counseling processes, but there is little moral difficulty for the counselor in doing what he or she has been asked to do.

Ethical difficulties can emerge when a person comes for counseling with no expressed desire for religious or moral considerations to be part of the process. If a person is distraught and very needy, immediate support and direct help must be given in the crisis without bringing in other considerations. When the crisis has been resolved and the person becomes stronger and wishes to continue counseling, the counselor can then introduce other factors, which may make a difference. In negotiating the implicit and perhaps informal contract for the counseling still to come, the counselor should give some minimal description in ordinary language of his or her methods and framework of values.

It is more honest to be open at the beginning, since there can actually be no completely value-free counseling; the person in a counseling relationship has a right to know what his or her chosen helper will generally think to be helpful. But barring special requests, helpers should not go into so much detail about their own approaches that attention is distracted from the person who seeks help. Only so much information can be assimilated at once, and at the beginning of counseling it is important that support, empathy, and full explorations of the presenting problems should be established, rather than ideological discourse.

Only when intimacy has been fully developed will the question of ethical confrontation arise. While it can be true that a counselor can give unconditional positive regard to a person, it is hardly possible or morally right to give positive affirmation to morally wrong things a person does or plans to do. Each counselor's moral framework will include a range of acceptable or indifferent acts that can be viewed with detachment, but there are limits to what the counselor can silently accept without confrontation and an expression of moral disapproval. Otherwise the counselor becomes morally complicit with wrongdoing and risks bringing moral harm to the person he or she is seeking to help.

If the counselor learns in a counseling session that the client intends to endanger another, there are both moral and legal mandates for breaking confidentiality. Threats of harm to another or reports of child abuse are in some states incidents that a counselor is required to report to authorities. Here the ethics of discretion and the need for a sense of security and safety in the helping relationship give way to the universal principles of equal protection from harm for all in the community.

Today in theories of helping others "toughlove" is generally approved, and counselors are warned not to enable or facilitate another person's flight from responsibility or the real consequences of his or her behavior. A completely accepting, morally blind approach to inappropriate behavior can label all deviance as sickness beyond a person's control and does many individuals a disservice. Persons who can know the difference between right and wrong and who are able to hear and understand a moral admonition should be morally admonished when doing wrong—as tactfully, prudently, and effectively as possible.[14] If part of what a helping relationship conveys is a better model of living, then the counselor as moral agent who can make judgments is a model of qualities that the person needs to identify with and incorporate.

The point is that self-respect and self-love are built upon moral agency and commitment to certain standards of behavior. Violating these standards within the counseling relationship or in the outside environment will create harm to self and others, as well as other unpleasant practical consequences. Morals, discipline, and personal happiness are interrelated, so it is false to pretend that they are not. The special relationship of counseling allows one to be uninhibited and free in reflecting upon the good and the bad in one's self and life, so the moral dimension cannot be avoided after a distraught, crisis stage has passed. Certainly, traditional Christian love always includes a confrontation with the truth as well as tenderness, comfort, support, and forgiveness.

Ethical confrontation may be unavoidable, but religious conversion and persuasion are not. I do not think that a religiously believing counselor should try to convert an unbelieving client or one of different beliefs. It is one thing to confront a moral wrong and give moral judgments of the unacceptable, but it is another to try to persuade a person being helped to convert. The inequality in power and the person's tendency to overestimate a helper in counseling make such efforts suspect. The person being helped is not free enough or in equal enough circumstances to put up a fair fight. (The same inequality of power produces a taboo on sexual encounters in counseling, which have been seen as similar to incest.) It takes a detached, free set of circumstances to garner the free assent of a fully integrated person. Unless spiritual counseling has been explicitly contracted for, a counselor should explicitly not seek to persuade a person of religious truth while counseling.

This restraint, however, does not mean that Christian counselors should not try to love those they help and feel free to use spiritual means to help the healing process. A believing counselor can pray for those he or she wishes to help and perhaps even fast or make sacrifices. These efforts should usually best be kept private, since otherwise they might seem to be coercive, manipulative techniques. Only when the helper and the person seeking help are fellow members of a believing community can praying together in public be appropriate. The counselor certainly should not sanction any laying on of hands with directed prayer unless a prayer community is involved, which is part of the group of believers.

Privately religious people who counsel unbelievers can pray for those they desire to help, and they can ask guidance. They may pray and hope the unbelievers will be healed and even that they accept the good news. But tact and respect for the person's present convictions recommend reticence. If the person expresses spiritual interests and wants to go further than remedial problem solving in counseling, the safest course for a counselor would be to recommend another trusted person or minister for further help in the client's spiritual journey. In the past unfortunate stories were current of missionaries converting "rice Christians," who came for periodic rations of food; no one would want to have a modern equivalent in which pastors gained converts mainly through their therapeutic counseling skills.

## Personal Ethical Challenges Confronting the Pastoral Counselor

Counselors have to employ an ethics of intimacy and discretion in regard to themselves and their own spiritual well-being. The power that one can wield in a helping relationship is accompanied by dangers. Again and again in personal intimate encounters, counselors must use themselves as self-conscious instruments, calling upon their emotional resources and shrewd social skills to be able to intervene, or interpret, or say the right thing at the right time. They must establish rapport and empathy with other people and truly listen while at the same time reflecting upon what they hear with the analytic "third ear."

The counseling process is draining and demanding, for its intimacy is unlike other personal intimacies that give mutual comfort and self-directed satisfactions. Intimacy in counseling is unselfishly directed to the other person's needs. If there is conflict or confrontation, it is not the simple, uncontrolled, spontaneous conflict one can have with a peer, whose strength and well-being can be counted on. A counselor in a helping relationship always has a double responsibility, careful monitoring both of one's self and the other person. These stressful circumstances in which the emotions and the self must be actively engaged have been called the problems of "the managed heart." It takes a toll to call publicly and continually upon those intimate resources that usually are reserved for private life.

It is important for counselors to recognize these stresses and try to avoid depleting their personal energies and lives. Those who would help others in arduous, intimate counseling relationships must take care of their own needs for intimacy and renewal. Counselors need proper physical care and many resources for meeting their own needs for love, growth, and spiritual refreshment. Regular times of retreat and sabbatical withdrawal from counseling may be required to prevent the troubling symptoms of mechanical depersonalization or attacks of psychic numbing that can occur when helpers are emotionally overloaded and overworked.

Many positive things have been said about the idea of "the wounded healer," but this concept has to be more carefully examined.[15] The question is whether personal weaknesses and limitations can impede or help the counseling relationship. Some have claimed that as in Alcoholics Anonymous, the weaknesses or flaws of the counselor can be an aid in helping others who are weak and needy. My own conclusion is different and more qualified: personal reflection on *past* failures that have been overcome can help counselors, but at the actual time of counseling, personal flaws and weaknesses simply dilute the counselor's effectiveness. It is the *sober* alcoholics who can help their fellows stay sober, not those still drinking.

A counselor needs to be as wise and virtuous and free from flaws and self-deception as possible. The person being helped will sense hypocrisy or selfish egotism and be less willing to follow the model or guidance of such a person. The need for personal integrity and practicing what one preaches is all the more important if the counselor is a pastor known to those he or she is trying to help. The reaction of the person being helped to the character and personality of the counselor is all-important in effective counseling. The healer should be as whole, healthy, competent, and virtuous as possible. And it also helps to be happy.

The temptations of persons who have institutional authority and personal power are subtle and can quickly lead to self-deception. Vigilance is necessary to live the life of virtue in the counseling vocation—as in any calling in which one may take pride in doing good while one is doing one's work well. So although humble consciousness of past wounds that have been sustained can be an asset to a helper, the fewer wounds and the more present strength, the better.

Many counselors have become seriously impaired in the process of helping others and yet have been able to rationalize and deny their own problems. Counselors who are responsible for others must take greater care to search out peers and superiors who can scrutinize and counsel them. When one knows of counselors who are impaired, who are denying their weaknesses and beginning to harm self and others, it is a moral duty to change a situation in which they can operate freely.

At the other extreme, it is important to realize that even the most vigilant, virtuous, dedicated, and competent counselors will meet failures in their work. The suffering caused by the inability fully to help others is part of the cross of counseling. This suffering and the constant reminder of one's limitations can take its own toll. The temptation is to become overdetached from outcomes and develop a defensive professionalism. It takes great wisdom and energy to keep caring and giving one's all, while at the same time yielding up all the fantasies of omnipotent rescue that bedevil helping professionals.

If counselors cannot let go of their own will to control and cure, then there will come the moment in which they begin to blame the client for not getting better or not getting better faster. The personal desire to exert all-out efforts in order to relieve suffering can easily be transformed into a personal need to exert force in order not to suffer the pain of failure. Counseling, like parenting, tests its practitioners in the depths of their own character. Effective counselors cannot retreat from their personal investment, so they remain vulnerable to the pain and costs of an intimacy that may fail.

In the end, the intimacy of the counseling relationship is both its strongest and most problematic characteristic. Intimacy provides the counselor the potential to help, but like all exercises of power, it has its personal and ethical dangers. Love in action is never simple.

## CHAPTER 6

# Healing in a Theological Perspective

## Jasper N. Keith Jr.

THE CONTEXT OF PASTORAL COUNSELING PUTS SOME PARA-
meters on both the practice of healing and the perspective of
theology. The fact that these reflections are those of a pastoral
theologian identified with the Presbyterian-Reformed tradition both defines and limits this essay. The question prompt-
ing all theological perspectives is, "What is the living God
whom we know in Christ through the Holy Spirit and in the
Bible doing and saying in our time, here and now, where we
have to think and live as Christians?"[1] I hope in this essay to
make a contribution to that inquiry.

I will begin with John Smith's experience of pain in his
chest. From that human situation I will offer some views of
healing in present-day society. Then I will define pastoral
counseling and describe some of the aspects of healing and
some theological perspectives implicit in Smith's experience.
Finally, I will relate Smith's experience to an understanding
of wholeness and healing within scripture and will consider
to what extent our understanding of healing has been affected
by these biblical and theological perspectives.

The Rev. Jasper N. Keith, Jr., S.T.D., is professor of pastoral care and
counseling at Columbia Theological Seminary, Atlanta.

## A Delineation of Health

Reflecting on a scene in a typical doctor's office, especially that of a general practitioner, may yield a definition of some concepts of healing.

### John Smith's Visit to His Doctor

The office nurse squeezed Smith into an already tight schedule because he sounded quite concerned about some chest pains, a racing heart, some light-headedness and weakness in his legs. The doctor paid attention to these symptoms and employed the technology available in order to make as accurate a diagnosis as possible. An electrocardiogram was done, blood was drawn, blood pressure and pulse rate were taken. The results made the doctor suspicious of a possible myocardial infarction. Smith was hospitalized, placed in the coronary-care unit, and monitored. The doctor prescribed medication and ordered other diagnostic tests. The medical team carried out the treatment and made further tests.

At that time Smith was considered to be ill. He had not yet been identified as the "myocardial infarction in bed no. 4," but he might have been, after the tests were completed. He did not know if he had a diseased artery, but he knew he was "dis-eased." Whatever was happening to him, he was not his usual self. For some reason communication between the systems of his body had broken down, and he was out of balance and experiencing disharmony. He was fearful not only of what the problem might be but also of whether it could be corrected. For these moments Smith's world had narrowed down to a coronary-care unit, and the laser beam of eternity was aimed at his heart. Whatever tests it took, he wanted the doctor to give him a clean bill of health.

Within forty-eight hours the doctor, with the help of technology, determined that there had been no heart attack.

The high blood pressure would be controlled by medication, by a thirty-pound weight loss, and by a sodium-free diet. Smith was advised to stop smoking and begin a light exercise routine. To lower his cholesterol he was to start a low-fat diet and consume oat bran and niacin.

Smith was discharged from the hospital feeling "like a new man," and ready to go back to work. But is Smith healthy? Is he well? How has he been healed, if he has been?

### Exploring Views of Health

What views of sickness and health informed Smith's awareness of his own condition?

*Health as the Goal of Life*. First, it does not appear that Smith has been caught up in the popular pursuit of health as the goal of human life. But many people in present-day American society are devoted to that goal. Health, like a new house, a new automobile, or a computer, is the consumer's right. The absence of pain, the unhindered ability to pursue happiness, and the assurance that death will not come prematurely are powerful goals of much behavior. Health spas, health foods, health aids, and health products are big business. People assume that somewhere there is the right diet, the right exercise, and the right pill for every excess pound, flabby muscle, and irritating ailment. The good nutritionist or therapist or physician is the one who can relieve the pain and provide the quick fix with as little effort as possible on the part of the consumer.

This self-centered assumption promotes the illusion that one can stay fit, look younger, eliminate illness, and postpone death until further notice. This overarching pursuit of health motivates the behavior, relationships, and commitments of a great multitude of people.

*Health as a Subject of Chronic Complaint*. Second, neither

does it appear that Smith was a chronic complainer about his miseries. He wasn't jumping from one doctor to the next until he found one who would confirm his diagnosis and collude with his deduction that life is a bitch, he has been cheated, and someone ought to make it right for him. He doesn't sit in one spot day and night imagining one pain after another or convincing himself that he is suffering every disorder portrayed by some characters on television. No, Smith is a lot like my grandmother; he goes to a doctor only as a last resort.

Fifty years ago people went to doctors because they were ill, too ill to function. Nowadays, people go to doctors because they are "not well," because they feel vague dis-comfort or dis-ease. But "not being well" in grannie's mind was not far from being healthy. And "not being well" can occur as a result of biological, social, psychological, economic, or spiritual problems, only a small portion of which a medical doctor has either the technology to diagnose or the expertise to treat. "Not being well" could be treated by a golf game with a friend or by a commission bonus, job promotion, or even an encouraging word from a supervisor. "Not being well" is different from "being ill." And on this morning, Smith was ill, too ill to take a shower, much less to go to work.

*Health as a Subject of Ignorance*. Third, it seems likely that Smith had given little thought to health, his own or anyone else's, until the morning he awoke with pains in his chest. He understood the malfunction of his body about as much as he did the breakdown of his Honda. He has to depend on the knowledge and expertise of skilled technicians to discover what is wrong and to keep both body and car running smoothly. He has insurance to cover the breakdown of either, and the proper functioning of both is his consumer right. He pays for services rendered, and he demands customer satisfaction. The good technician has the best possible equipment to make an accurate diagnosis of trouble. The good mechanic goes into the body or the engine; removes, replaces, or repairs the faulty part; and makes Smith or his car operational again. Many people have a simplistic understanding of health: if they can function, they are healthy.

In a sense Smith reflects a view of reality that has dominated the Western world since the philosophy of René Descartes, the mathematical theory of Isaac Newton, and the scientific methodology of Francis Bacon. Matter is the basis of all physical existence, and it is governed by laws of motion. Rational thought, including logic, is the way to know and control matter. The reduction of complex phenomena into their building blocks of matter and the analysis of the mechanisms through which they are connected are the methods of knowing and changing matter.[2]

These perspectives powerfully influence the biomedical understanding of sickness and health. Physical disease is caused by an invasion from outside the human organism. Patients are helpless victims of external and unpredictable disease processes that strike at random. The mind of someone other than the patient has to analyze the parts, isolate and identify the microorganism of infection, diagnose the cause, and treat the malfunction. Whether it is bacteria, a virus, or some foreign substance such as dust, asbestos, or chemical compounds, the culprit comes from outside the person and invades a hapless victim.

These perceptions of external causality relieve the person of responsibility for whatever is wrong with one of the parts of the mechanical body and thus for his or her sickness, healing, or health. But these causal perspectives assume that a rational explanation can be found for the problem and a logical solution can be prescribed.

*Health as the Absence of Illness*. Fourth, many people see health simply as the absence of illness or physical disability. I was visiting a frail, little old woman slumped in her wheelchair. Her hands were knotted with arthritis and her ankles seemed ready to burst through the swollen, stretched skin. I

said, "How are you?" "Can't you see how I am?" she snarled.
Near her a bedridden man fighting lung cancer for his every
breath, moaned, "When you got your health, you've got
everything." Like John Smith, these patients, too, were view-
ing health as the absence of illness or of physical disability.
Take away their productive ability, reduce their world to a
bed or a wheelchair, and they feel they have no health, that
life is unfair, and that they've been given the short end of the
stick. If they could, they'd strike for a better cut of the gross
national product, too, because a well-running machine is as
much their right as it is Smith's or anyone else's; and if it's
not guaranteed in the Constitution of these United States, it
ought to be.

*Health as Having Things Right.* Fifth, of course, there are
some other people who do not appear to have anything
mechanically wrong with them. But after a brief time in their
company, you sense that something is not "right" with them.
They may say that they feel fine, even that they are well. But
their spirit is sour, their attitude is bad, and their quality of
life is not up to snuff. One wonders what set of values activates
them, what emotional blockages inhibit them, and what fears
and anxieties prejudice them. It is more than difficult to apply
to them the term "healthy."

*Health as Wholeness.* Sixth, I have known some people
who were seriously sick, severely disabled, and diagnosed as
critically ill yet whose health and wholeness shone like a
beacon on a dark seashore. Dottie suffered from multiple
sclerosis. She jerked constantly from muscle spasms. The pain
was like a hot poker being pushed up her leg. But weekly,
members of her church transported her for counseling because she wanted "to maintain her sense of humor and
become who she was." After she and I had established a
trusting relationship, she gave me a paper weight on which
she painted: "My cow is dead; so I don't need any of your

bull." She said she wanted my acceptance, the integrity of my faith in God, and my Christian hope to undergird our human relationship.

In my understanding Dottie incarnated Jurgen Moltmann's definition of health: "True health is the strength to live, the strength to suffer, and the strength to die. Health is not a condition of my body; it is the power of my soul to cope with the varying conditions of that body."[3] Health for people like Dottie is not a fixed and static state but a venturesome, dynamic equilibrium in which life is valued and relationships are embraced. Health is not some attainable goal, but it is some dynamic, often unselfconscious pursuit that will never be satisfied in this life. Health takes on the connotations of "creatively becoming" and "being made whole."

## Health as Everything That Affects the Organism

Smith wanted the doctor "to give him a clean bill of health." The doctor looked to the marvelous world of technology to find causes of dis-ease. Sometimes an accurate diagnosis can be made about a cause, and a doctor can alleviate illness, palliate pain, or treat a disease process, thereby restoring one to a former or better state of physical existence. But no one can give Smith a clean bill of health. Health is a much more inclusive and elusive phenomenon. For health encompasses everything that has an impact on the human organism, and the state of one's health includes far more than the mere absence of disease or infirmity.

If we consider the health of entire populations or the health of Smith, medical interventions have comparatively little impact. In my lifetime the decline of infectious diseases, such as tuberculosis, has been due chiefly to improved nutrition and hygiene, which in turn resulted from advances in agriculture and the science of epidemiology. In appraising health Thomas McKeown suggests that "We owe the improvements, not to what happens when we are ill, but to the fact that we do not so often become ill; and we remain well, not because of specific measures such as vaccination and immunization, but because we enjoy a higher standard of nutrition and live in a healthful environment."[4] Promotion of health involves such factors as safe housing, purified water supplies, efficient waste disposal (especialy nuclear waste disposal), safety regulations about food, immunization programs, improvement of the environment, and balance of the ecological systems.

Smith is no doubt grateful for what the medical doctor, through technology, has learned about him. And he probably found the bill easy to pay because he had adequate insurance coverage. He may now join the chorus of a larger public that applauds medical technology in spite of its escalating costs. He may be appreciative of the biomedical model with its primary focus on diagnosis, causal treatment, and crisis intervention. *But to conclude that he is healthy or that he has been healed is to betray a deficient vision of human life and a myopic view of healing.*

### A Ministry of Pastoral Counseling

But there is more to the story of Smith. Some months after his hospitalization, his wife expressed concern about his welfare to their pastor. Smith was not taking his medication regularly. He had stopped exercising, was consuming more alcohol, and still smoked two packs of cigarettes a day. He was still having some tightness in his chest and was increasingly irritable with her and their teenage boys. Mrs. Smith wondered if the pastor could call on Smith.

Before the pastor could schedule lunch into his tight schedule, Smith was back in the doctor's office. This time the doctor took the approach of a listening physician. After a caring, straight talk with Smith, the physician acknowledged that they were dealing with a more complex mystery than a simple physical problem. It was a lifestyle rather than an organic malfunction. What was affecting Smith was more vague, more complex than a germ one could isolate under a microscope. It was more like principalities and powers running loose within the culture, stressing out middle-aged corporate executives. The doctor referred Smith to a pastoral counselor.

What technology will I as this professional counselor employ? What will be my worldview, philosophy of life, theory of personality, understanding of disease? Chances are that Smith will still be looking for a "quick fix"—some ways to modify his behavior, some relaxation techniques, maybe some tapes he can listen to as he battles the traffic of the freeway. He is likely to declare up front that he doesn't want "any of that religious talk." So, what understanding of healing will guide me as pastoral counselor? To answer that question, I must first define pastoral counseling.

### Definition of Pastoral Counseling

Pastoral counseling is one expression of the church's ministry of pastoral care. Pastoral counseling is usually rendered by one who is theologically educated, ecclesiastically ordained, and publicly identified and accountable as a member of the clergy.[5]

A pastoral-counseling relationship is usually initiated by the troubled person. The stated need is likely to reveal how that person is experiencing alienation from his or her faith, estrangement from other significant persons, or separation from some dimensions of his or her own history or all of these. If a relationship of trust can be established between the troubled person and the pastoral counselor, the person will have a supportive structure that will "enable the person once again to draw nourishment from the on-going processes of life. In this sense, pastoral counseling is expendable, its only goal being to arrive at the point where such an atypical relationship is no longer needed."[6]

In order to underscore the "pastoral" dimension of pastoral counseling, Wayne Oates described it as a "spiritual conversation"[7] and as "the God-in-relation-to-persons consciousness."[8] Ed Thornton saw pastoral counseling as "preparing the way for divine-human encounter,"[9] and he described "salvation" as of ultimate concern and "health" as of a penultimate order. Seward Hiltner contended that pastoral care and counseling provided operational data that could contribute to a constructive, pastoral theology.[10] Thomas Oden made attempts to build a bridge between pastoral counseling and some contemporary theologians.[11] More recently, both Wayne Oates[12] and Don Browning[13] have called attention to the ethical aspects of pastoral counseling. Undergirding these descriptions of the uniqueness of pastoral counseling is their agreement with what Paul Tillich called the ultimate concern for persons: namely, the awareness of God as ultimate reality. For it is that awareness of God that makes counseling pastoral.

I am in basic agreement with these perspectives of my colleagues, and I am deeply appreciative of them. I believe that the pastoral counselor must identify primarily with that theological heritage developed through a long history of the caring community, first recorded in the scriptures and then explicated by the saints. Further, I think the pastoral counselor must accept the symbolic and representative dimensions of the pastoral office. For pastoral counseling takes place within the commonwealth of eternal life as we have received it from God. It is this awareness of God as ultimate reality in the concrete human situation that makes care giving and counseling both pastoral and Christian.

Given these pastoral and theological perspectives, pastoral counseling is an exercise of faith, hope, and love. For the person of faith, no encounter is accidental. For the person of hope, every encounter has meaning. For the person of love, all encounters give rise to the most fundamental questions of theology: questions of sin and salvation, guilt and forgiveness, alienation and reconciliation, justification and sanctification, and finally, of life and death. Every encounter is potentially a way to a new discovery of one's self and of God.

Pastoral theology deals with human situations. Ideally this operational theology[14] is congruent with our dogmatic, systematic, and biblical theology, but it may also inform and reform what we say we believe. In any event, in the presence of troubled persons, the counselor's theological questions and formulations are more than theoretical. For "living human documents" existentially call for a caring response, and they inevitably force us prayerfully to discern the ways of God, who is still acting in human history through interpersonal relationships.

If the supreme revelation of God was given to the world in a personal incarnation, then personality is raised to a level of highest regard. If God's salvific work of redemption and reconciliation is done through the person and work of the Lord Jesus Christ, then personal relationships are raised to a level of greatest importance. If God's purpose is such that we who are in Christ are to bear witness of Christ's person, if we are ambassadors through whom God is making an appeal to persons, if we are given the personal message and are entrusted with the very interpersonal ministry of reconciliation, then pastoral counseling is a most personal venture of faith. The God we want to know and serve can be discovered afresh in the encounters between us as counselors and the human documents with whom we are called to relate carefully and caringly.

Thus far I have defined pastoral counseling as a ministry of the church and as an exercise of faith, hope, and love. I have suggested some theological dimensions that undergird the unique "pastoral" aspects of pastoral counseling. Admittedly, this definition is ideal, and the crux of the matter is how it can be made operational. What would pastoral counseling with Smith look like? What follows describes a portion of that process.

## Description of Pastoral Counseling

From what we now know about Smith, we can expect him to be a bit anxious about or resistant to this counseling business and not yet ready to assume much personal responsibility for his predicament. More than likely he will expect the pastoral counselor to be another problem solver and will be hoping for a quick fix. He may be prepared for a battery of personality tests, some kind of diagnosis, some treatment regimen, and maybe even some prescription drugs. After all, he has a problem that needs a solution.

### The "Who" Question

But the initial interview doesn't begin with either a battery of tests or a barrage of "what" questions. Instead, I begin with a "who" question: "Good morning. I know your name is John Smith, but I'd like to know more about who you are."

For the pastoral counselor there are both practical and theological reasons for beginning with a "who" question. Practically, the counselor wants to demonstrate openness to establishing an interpersonal relationship and to clarify that his or her expertise is as a relational person rather than as a problem solver. Theologically, the counselor perceives Smith to be made in the image of God for relatedness in freedom with love and justice.

Therefore, to begin with "what" questions simply is not personal enough. For "what" questions do not treat Smith as a subject for relationship so much as they make him an object to be analyzed, studied, or observed. "What" questions have already made him a potential cardiac patient; but "who" questions reveal a stressed out, disillusioned corporate executive; an angry, disappointed father; and a bored, trapped husband whose despair, loneliness, and isolation are breaking his spirit. "What" questions explain parts of a machine that may break under pressure; "who" questions unveil a weary, exasperated person in mid-life who is wondering, What's it all about? "What" questions limit him to whatever is contained within the boundary of his skin; "who" questions connect him to those significant relationships that comprise the essence of his existence in God's cosmos.

Theologically, I already have a partial answer to the "who" questions. For whoever else Smith is, he is a personal *thou*. Not a mechanical it, but a relational *thou*, who has entered the counselor's field of awareness and sphere of relating. In a very real sense, Smith *is* his relationships. He has become who he is as he has interacted within a network of significant relationships. Both his sickness and his health take place within that network. He will become human only in and through relatedness, and he will alter his being as he gains strength to do so from some significant relationships. Now he has the option of entering into a relationship with me as his counselor. And the quality of this relationship will affect Smith this day and every day for the rest of his life. I operate on the premise that relationships matter and that wholeness comes only through loving and just relatedness with God, others, and self.

The ministering person must continually ask "who" questions as the first and primary questions of ministry. Regardless of the particularity of each person's story, a basic part of every answer to the "who" questions is this theological truth: "We are people of God, subjects of God's love. That's who we are; that's who we all are." Other givens are that we are human creatures made in the image of God for relatedness in freedom with love and justice; that we are endowed with a certain human dignity that entails certain relationships, rights, and responsibilities; and that we are called to be a pilgrim people of the faithful and purposive God and to be witnesses to God's suffering love and liberating power. The pastoral counselor has a skeletal answer to the "who" questions, but only Smith can enflesh it with his unique story.

"Good morning, sir. Who are you?" That is the first question in the ministry of those who represent the triune God. "I know your name, but I would like to know who you are, with whom you have become, and with whom you now belong." Smith fumbled and stuttered, but the counselor continued asking different "who" questions until Smith had revealed much of who he is in and through his significant relations.[15]

I hope you have heard this pastoral theologian affirming the theological dimensions inherent in the "who" questions. If so, I trust you will understand why I believe them to be the first and foremost questions in a ministry of pastoral counseling. By the time the "who" questions were answered, I had already heard some of the answers to the "what" questions. I probably did not need to ask them, but I asked them anyway because I wanted to communicate my respect for Smith. Additionally, I wanted to put the responsibility and choice for the counseling process where it rightfully belongs—with the recipient.

## The "What" Questions

Before the initial interview was ended, I asked: "What's happening with you? What brings you here today?" "What prompted your coming to see me?" and "What are you wanting from this relationship?" Note both the open-endedness and the specificity of those questions.

Note also how they acknowledge that the responsible choice belongs with Smith. They also communicate implicitly a genuine respect for Smith as one who will be his own person and rely on his own wise counsel. That invitation-command is intentional because I want Smith to trust himself and to trust himself in this relationship. I am also inviting Smith to overcome his doubt and shame about himself by affirming what he wants and needs.

Another reason for these particular "what" questions is that they focus on the present moment in the relationship between me as pastoral counselor and Smith. The questions may create anxiety or embarrassment, but they also begin the "therapeutic alliance." More important, they underscore the healing factor in the counseling process—the interpersonal relationship. Whatever else pastoral counseling is, it is an interpersonal relationship! And without a certain quality of interpersonal relating, pastoral counseling is simply impossible. As early as possible, then, I want to create a safe enough space that Smith can talk about this relationship and my importance to him. If this is done, both the resistance and the transference will be reduced, and the interpersonal relationship will be fostered.

Also, these questions announce the hopeful prospects for change. For they assume that Smith is actively participating in and taking responsibility for the altering of his life situation. He will also, it is hoped, discern that I as his counselor trust his capacity to choose between alternatives and to change what he wants to change. That trust implicitly connotes respect for Smith and hope for the relationship between him and me. My questions recognize the human dignity of Smith and seek to tap into that image of God in which Mr. Smith was created in freedom for love and right relatedness.

Finally, these "what" questions confront Smith's perception of his struggle. His problem is not external to him; he is his own worst enemy. But neither is this struggle all his doing. He exists in a family, a corporation, a community, and now in a counseling relationship. He has decisions to make, actions to take, responsibilities to assume in all these systems; but perhaps he can begin to see that he is less alone, less isolated, and more in relationship.

Those are some of the reasons for the "what" questions. Discernment of what is happening here is the second task of pastoral counseling. One cannot respond to a need until one knows what the need is.[16] But discerning the need in some instances is no simple matter. And, in the end, only Smith can reveal what is presently happening with him and how he is feeling about and utilizing this relationship.

I could have asked the "what" questions in the following manner: "What is the *issue* here calling for *my* discernment? What is the *problem* here calling for *my* solution? What is the *crisis* here calling for *my* intervention? What is the *panic* here calling for *my* structure? What is the *dilemma* here calling for *my* guidance? What is the *predicament* here calling for *my* compassion?" This kind of questioning emphasizes the ability of the counselor. These questions assume that Smith is a helpless victim who is now the counselor's responsibility. In the wisdom of the counselor, Smith is to be taken care of. Now, for me, that is as far from reality as the south pole is from the north. And I do not want to participate in any such grandiosity regarding myself or any such denigration of another human being.

Also, as with the "who" questions, I have a partial answer to the "what" questions. I know that whatever else is true, Smith, like the rest of us, is caught between what he was made potentially to be and what he is essentially. Like the rest of us he has known some forms of bondage to sin, some aspects of deliverance, some relative freedom, and some partial experience of wholeness. Additionally, Smith, like the rest of us, is dying and will one day know assuredly that he is mortal. Although he is made for relatedness with God, Smith is among those creatures who can answer God (either in defiance or in trust) and can converse with God (either in praise or argument).

After listening to his story, I have good reason to believe that Smith has reached that state of existence in which he knows estrangement and experiences a loneliness that is about to make him cynical and bitter. He has all but lost the courage to be; and he is experiencing poignantly the anxiety of his finitude. He is close to experiencing meaninglessness and despair. He seems on the verge of the sloth (*ahgadia*) that cries: "I don't care. What's the use of it all?" Experientially, he is a sinner in need of grace that finds expression in relatedness and community.

I believe that the business of the church consists chiefly of pastoral-care givers, clergy or lay, being vulnerable in their concerns for others, offering costly grace and making relationships matter, and communicating that nothing can ultimately separate any of us from the love of God. But pastoral-care givers must also know that there is a very thin line that separates "us," the ministers, from "them," those that need support. There, we too have been, could be, and would be, except for the grace of God and the love of our significant relationships. And even with those blessings, we rightfully confess: "We have left undone those things which we ought to have done; and we have done those things we ought not to have done; and there is no health in us."

The business of the church, including the work of pastoral counseling, is ever done by "forgiven sinners" who have their own problems of unhealth. While as counselors we dare to care for others, we cannot escape the symptoms of our own frustrated longing for relationships of trust with God and neighbor. We are in ·need of God's gracious forgiveness and acceptance as everyone is. Our relating and loving are pale reflections of God's justice and love. The most any of us can do is bear witness to God, who alone is truly just and truly loves, and who is now suffering with and liberating all of us. For us and for them, the path to true wholeness is always the way of relatedness. A wise writer of scripture described the church of forgiven sinners in this manner: "For we are all members one of another."[17] And we are more alike than we are different!

Perhaps you did not need me to make those comments, but for my sake, I need continually to say them. Having stated them, I can now describe what healing looks like in pastoral counseling. You will understand that whatever else I say must be heard in light of this acknowledgment that I am a "forgiven sinner."

In discussing the "who" and "what" questions, I have emphasized the centrality of the personal relationship being developed by two humans made in the image of God for relatedness in freedom with love and justice. That theological construct is basic to my understanding of who we are and what we do. I am concerned that these "who" and "what" questions be grasped as theological and theoretical rather than technical or strategic, for they are full of theological meaning. In addition, Smith's responses provide data for understanding who and what he brings to this relationship as well as some of the resistances one might anticipate in relating with him. In this context, we now consider how healing took place in and through this interpersonal relationship.

## Healing Through Pastoral Counseling

We know that Smith is experiencing job-related stress, that he is not sharing his feelings with anyone, and that he has not found much meaning in who he is. He is the abandoned, only son of a deceased, drunken war hero, and he is the caretaker of a dependent mother, who is a rejected widow. He is also the husband of a dependent woman whose primary joy is in being a doting mother and a devoted church worker. Smith also is cut off from any significant relationships in which there is mutual care. For too many years he has assumed the role of caretaker, and he is close to exhaustion.

A healing relationship will involve entrusting himself to another, discovering his own need for dependence, and being accepted as the "needy child" he is, rather than the caretaking "little adult" others have needed him to be. This process will entail a temporary regression, maybe some anguishing expression of shame and anger, and some rebellious assertion of his need to be free of all these caretaking responsibilities. His process will probably involve some powerful transference material that may be negative toward a male figure. How then shall I as pastoral counselor facilitate a healing process with Smith?

### Empathic Listening

First, the continual work of pastoral counseling is empathic listening to Smith's unique story, his feelings about it, and the meanings he can make from it. I am limited by and dependent upon what the client communicates. The continual work is listening with the ears and watching with the eyes what the client reveals.

As often as I was able really to listen to Smith, I implicitly endowed him with power, because I was taking him seriously. But sometimes I resisted listening for two reasons. If I was really to listen to Smith, I had first to be willing to listen to myself. Inextricably bound to my ability to listen to another and to listen to myself is my sense of self-value and self-acceptance. For me to listen to myself is to engage the most threatening aspect of my being. But also, if I am really to listen to another and to myself, I must be willing to be informed and reformed by what I hear. The extent to which I reach out to Smith and let Smith in to me will depend, in part, on my ability to risk allowing my view of myself, Smith, and the world to change. That openness to whatever comes is anxiety provoking; and sometimes I resist that anxiety.

When I can get beyond my own anxiety, listening entails being truly present with another without trying to correct, change, inform, or do anything but listen to his or her perceptions and feelings. When listening to another, one has to discern between facts and meanings. Facts are "what-has-happened-to-me" information. Meanings are "how what has happened to me affects me." Meanings are usually expressed in emotional words such as afraid, scared, worried, concerned, hurt, upset, frustrated, angry. Beyond the emotional words lie the significant meanings, the depth dimensions of life.

Listening to persons' stories, their feelings about their stories, and the meanings they put into them, is to establish a kind of solidarity with those persons, to become involved in their predicament, and to suffer with them through their crises. If the pastoral counselor listens with the ears and watches with the eyes, he or she may discover that healing comes through the person's having been heard.

## Asking the Right Question

Second, the timely work of pastoral counseling is asking the right question. I need to find out what Smith is asking of me. Most of the time people know what they want and will tell you if you ask them. Asking the right question at the right time is an indispensable skill in the art of caring. The answer that is given is largely determined by the question asked. And the next question is always a more significant art form than the last interpretation that was made. Asking the right questions at the right time is an art. The right, well-timed question compels a straight answer. Questions can help me know what Smith is expecting and wanting from me.

Open-ended questions are essential. They allow people room to back off, to reflect, to marshall their strengths, and to determine how much more they are willing for the counselor to hear, see, and know.

Additionally, questioning values the experiences, knowledge, feelings, and perceptions, of the other, takes them seriously, and indicates an openness to receiving from the other. In questioning, the I-over-you, I-smarter-than-you attitude is avoided, and the possibility of the person's becoming dependent on the counselor's advice and wisdom is diminished. Additionally, questioning stimulates the person's thinking, feeling, taking initiative, assuming responsibility, and coming to his or her own wise conclusion. Questioning facilitates healing as it increases awareness, freedom, relatedness, and self-transcendence.[18]

Up to this point, I have spent a large portion of time and energy listening to Smith and asking questions. But I listen to more than words about the past and ask for more than Smith's thoughts. I consider Smith's posture, facial expressions, blushes, and silences. I ask Smith about his fantasies and daydreams, his tender and aggressive feelings, what he is experiencing just now when he bit his lower lip or whitened his knuckles.

Slowly, but surely, the counselor and the client learn to talk with each other, enter each other's frame of reference, and share their feelings. Communication becomes more congruent; is expressed more in the first person, present tense; and takes on a straightforward, honest, trusting posture. Nothing is too sacred to be questioned, and nothing is too awful to express. Counselor and client cannot not communicate; they are ever communicating, but in this relationship there is increasing awareness about *what* is being communicated and how and when that communication occurs. There is healing in such transparent relating.

## Working in Depth

Once language and symbols are shared, the depth work of pastoral counseling can occur. When a person isn't expecting it, up from the depths come feelings of affection, annoyance, anger, anxiety, fear, guilt, joy, or shame. These powerful, frightening feelings make us ever so vulnerable. But they create pregnant moments of *kairos*—moments when the monstrous agony moans, aching sadness sobs, old wounds bleed, or a tornado of rage is unleashed. Chaos yet unnamed breaks through the repressed. Forgotten memories flood the mind and wreak havoc with an otherwise calm morning. Remembered experiences of malign abuse or of tender nurture tug at the heart, and life can never be the same again. Both the client and the counselor are at a loss for words. There is no language except that which is felt between them, and no symbols more adequate than the shared tears and deep sighs. In those awesome, grateful moments, both the person in need and the counselor experience the intimate work of pastoral counseling and the subsequent healing for each of them.

## The Interpretive Task

Then comes the tedious work, the interpretative task of making connections between the feelings and those events so that new meanings are forged. Carroll Wise described the essence of therapy and of redemption as "helping a person discover the depths of his own being and express this in symbols that carry vital meanings."[19] The connective task involves Smith's present life situation, his past experiences, his characteristic patterns of response, transference material, and the relationship between him and me as the counselor. Out of the connections made comes insight, and with the emergence of every insight, new responsibilities follow. If the connections aren't made and insight does not come, the counseling process degenerates into an endless, repetitive rehashing of the person's "problem."

## Discerning the Faith Questions

Finally, the unique work of counseling that is pastoral is discerning the faith questions in Smith's story. This work is about more than the meaning of Smith's particular story; it is what every story is finally all about. This is what my colleague John Patton describes as the "presumptuous" work of ministry; that is, the pastoral counselor's "suggesting what the story is all about."[20] In order for such suggestions to be helpful, the counselor must employ shared symbols, and the suggestions must emerge out of the quality of the relationship. I agree with Patton's perspective:

If the counseling relationship has moved to the point where the particularities of who I am as a person are as important as what the counselee needs me to represent, then I have the freedom to use whatever symbols come most naturally to me to describe the depth of human experience. Before that time, I feel bound to respond almost wholly to the counselee's world with very little brought in from outside.[21]

Suggestions of what his story and my story are in light of God's story is a uniqueness that makes counseling pastoral.

The pastoral counselor and the person being counseled respond to each other in and through that relationship as each is enabled by God and allowed by the other. They respond without infringing on the other's rights or sense of responsibility, without promising more than they could deliver but remaining faithful to whatever they promised. They respond by continually trusting each other and entrusting each other to the God who makes all things new.

In that faithful and loving process, Smith learned to communicate more effectively with me, his wife, his mother, his two sons, and some coworkers. He became increasingly aware of his feelings and more comfortable in expressing them. He has taken his sons to his father's grave and visited with some cousins. An aunt gave him some old family photographs of his father. He is encouraging his mother to be more related to his sisters. He and his wife have joined a tennis team, are attending a couples Sunday School class, and are occasionally have satisfactory sexual relations. He's gone fishing several times with an elder from the church.

Smith's blood pressure has returned to normal, and his cholesterol is low enough. He lost ten pounds and on most days he isn't too uptight to enjoy a good joke. He's different. He isn't the way he was. He knows that, and so do those who are close to him. But is he healed? Healthy? Well? He is better than before, but can I claim anything more for Smith or for myself?

At this point the excruciating pain in Smith's chest is gone, along with much of the stress, isolation, and despair. Smith is a more productive, enjoyable, integrated, whole person than he ever dared dream he could be. A therapeutic relationship enabled him to enjoy more freedom, love, and justice in human relatedness than he had ever experienced before. He discovered a well-spring of healing resources within his own person, and he made some tough, but responsible choices about what he would do with who he was and what he had been given. He has accepted acceptance and knows the gratitude of a man grasped by grace. In a worshiping community he confesses regularly that he is a "forgiven sinner" who is a subject of God's love.

But Smith is also a finite, limited creature, who is a being-unto-death. And it is that theological reality that must finally be considered.

## A Theological Perspective

To take a theological perspective is to address questions about the ultimate meaning of life in terms of God, to employ language that expresses one's awareness and perception of God. The only way humans can speak about God is through symbols, images, metaphors, and analogies. Behind each particular symbol is a particular experience of a particular community within a particular historical context.

For me to take a theological perspective is to discourse on the revelation of God in Jesus Christ through the Holy Spirit. In using those words I have identified myself with the Judeo-Christian heritage and affirmed my faith in that community's symbols of the triune God who is Creator, Redeemer, and Giver of life. I conceptualize with images learned from scripture, the historical documents of the holy catholic church, and the confessions of the Presbyterian-Reformed tradition.

I call myself Christian because my relation to God has been

deeply affected by the person and work of Jesus the Christ in human history and in my history. Additionally, I have committed myself to what I understand to have been the cause of Christ, namely, the reconciliation of humankind to God. That reconciliation includes the establishment of a new creation, which means the increase among humankind of the love of God and neighbor with justice and peace.

In the literature of pastoral care, there is the conception that healing is a "restoration to wholeness."[22] Two things are wrong with that conception. First it is a mistake to assume that there was once a "wholeness" in human existence. If it ever existed in some idyllic garden, it certainly didn't last long. Second, there is no possibility for a "restored wholeness" in this creaturely, finite life. At most, we are only "relatively whole," just as we are only "relatively free."

Smith wasn't restored to wholeness. He had never known a wholeness to which he could be restored. In fact, he was taken beyond what he had ever experienced in terms of human relatedness and well-being. But even that good place for Smith was far from "wholeness." It was more enjoyment of life than he had ever previously known, but he was still not whole, complete, perfect, or mature. He remained a "frail creature of the dust and feeble as frail."

Among human creatures, there are no paragons of health and wholeness, Charles Atlas and Jane Fonda not withstanding. We are mortal beings regardless of the bulk we put on our chests and biceps or the inches we take off our waists and buttocks. Each of us will die no matter how normal our blood pressure, cholesterol level, or weight may be. However contemporary society may try to define "health," there is truth in the confession that "there is no health in us" finite creatures.

Where then are health and wholeness to be found? In reply to this question, my colleague Walter Brueggemann said: "I don't know what I'd say, but I know where I'd begin. I'd begin with Exodus 15:17—'I, Yahweh, am your Healer.' That's where I'd begin." Of course, if we are to consider theological perspectives on anything, that is where we must begin every time—with God.

The Judeo-Christian communities have spoken of God as the Covenant Maker, the Creator, and the Redeemer. God is the initiator of the covenant, who thereby orders human relatedness. God is the power and source behind all that is created. God manifests goodness, mercy, steadfast love, and grace. Humankind exists and moves and has being in the grace of God, and humankind's fundamental relationship is with God.

### God the Covenant Maker and Creator

In the salvation history of the Israelites, the experience of the covenant came before the theological constructions of God as Creator and Redeemer. The questions in a theology of the covenant are, To whom are we related? Who has made promises? Who has issued commands? For the Israelites, the answer to that "who" question was, "Yahweh!" Yahweh had taken the initiative in establishing the covenent because Yahweh had chosen Israel and set her apart from other nations for a special purpose. The historical story that unfolds is one of the "mighty acts of Yahweh."

When that story unfolded, the Israelites were not asking metaphysical questions about the nature of ultimate reality. What mattered to them was Yahweh's personal relationship to Israel within history. Thus, Israel's God, Yahweh, is defined through verbs, experienced through actions and events, and conceived as a dynamic impulse who creates, ordains, limits, generates, forms, establishes, breaks down, and most happily covenants with Israel. Israel's faith was first confessed in the form of *Heilsgeschichte*—the story of Yahweh's mighty acts of salvation in Israel's history.[23]

When Yahweh was no longer acting as a mighty God of war, the theologians struggled to understand how their God was now acting in the history of Israel. The Creation stories written in the reign of Solomon (J source) and the Exile or later (P source) conceive God to be not only the God of Israel but also the sovereign Lord of all history and the Creator of all things and peoples in history. Later still, when the theologians put the canon of scripture together, the Creation stories were placed at the beginning because they perceived Creation as the starting point of their history with Yahweh.

In positing this doctrine of Creation, the writers of scripture were not asking metaphysical questions about their origins or ontological questions about being. Nor were they asking scientific questions about the causes that produced the heavens and the earth and all things therein. Rather they were asking about their ultimate security in a most frightening world, the meaning and destiny of their corporate existence. Their questions were "existential" and "relational." On what fundamental structure of relationship with Yahweh could they depend? Who or what ultimately determines life? Who or what is in charge here?

Such questions spring not so much from intellectual curiosity as from anxiety about the mystery of existence in which our whole being is involved. Such questions about the ultimate ground and meaning of life are peculiarly "religious." They search for faithful answers and healing solutions to human problems. They are uttered in a spirit of faith and trust more than in terms of logical proof or verification. They are asked out of personal turmoil and anxiety, out of trembling and dread, or out of frustration and futility.

To the anxious inquirer about existence, the Judeo-Christian faith responds: We are creatures of God dependent utterly upon God's sovereign will and steadfast love; and *history*, from beginning to end, is under the sovereign purpose of God. Therefore, there is no health, freedom, wholeness, or salvation except as God's reign is fulfilled and manifested.

The Hebrew word that comes closest to an Old Testament concept of health is *shalom*. It means a "wholeness, completeness, soundness, and well-being" and may be applied in every sphere of life whether physical, mental, spiritual, or individual, social, corporate.[24] Yahweh offers a covenant that will secure *shalom* for the people. True *shalom* comes from Yahweh alone, and only in God can humankind know wholeness in personal being and in corporate relatedness. Such *shalom* was not related primarily to healthy conditions of the physical body. And God's *shalom* is far more comprehensive than any present-day secular idea of wellness or welfare.

The issue that determined the Old Testament view of health was a human's relatedness to God. That relatedness was manifested by an obedience to God's law, and that obedience was a disclosure of the holiness and righteousness of human character as it reflected the nature of God. The supreme command of God to the covenant people was: "Be holy, because I, the Lord your God, am holy."[25] This relationship between God and the covenant people was dynamic, and it was to be expressed in their being and their actions. To the degree that the nature and will of Yahweh was so reflected, there was relative wholeness and derived health in the people of Yahweh.

### God the Redeemer

The sad fact of human history, however, is that the people did not keep the covenant or assume responsible stewardship of creation. Time and again, God would renew the covenant with a faithful remnant, and God's worship would order a corporate community. Some prophet might put forth a new vision of the covenant. But time and again, God's *shalom* was only partially realized, and the wholeness experienced was a pale reflection of the glory God had intended. Generation after generation, people's only hope was the assurance that God, who had created and covenanted with them, would in the end redeem them. They believed that deliverance and salvation, healing and wholeness, were entirely God's work of grace, not their own works of righteousness. God the Redeemer would have to act continually in their history if a society of love and justice were ever to become a reality. The faithful, steadfast loving God, who is beyond all human metaphors and continually makes all things new, would have continually to love and forgive willful, rebellious creatures who thwart God's intentions for wholeness.

It is the particular Christian perspective that God's new creation is already an historical reality in the person and work of Jesus the Christ through the Holy Spirit within the Christian church. God's new humanity is "created in Christ" and exists now in a new relation to God and therefore a new relation to one another.[26] The old is passing away; behold, the "newness of life" is, and is coming, and the Christian community is a part of that new ordering of creation and of humanity. New creatures in Christ are to be partners with God in the ordering of God's new creation.

The new covenant is one of grace under the lordship of Jesus the Christ, who, through his life and person, his death and resurrection, has forgiven human sin and thereby restored human beings freely to a right relationship with God. At the cost of suffering love, humanity is liberated and restored. The good news is that in Jesus Christ through the Spirit, we are forgiven and accepted. The ultimate word has been spoken: it is the word that we are justified and sanctified by God's grace through faith.

While Jesus revealed God to human beings, he also demonstrated what it is to be fully human, fully free, fully obedient, and fully loving. He faithfully reconciled humanity with the triune God. We are to manifest this reconciliation by maturing into the likeness of Christ as we are enabled to do so by his grace and power. He has entrusted the mediation of this reconciliation to us humans. To respond to this trust faithfully, we have to abandon all our own schemes and so trust God that we gratefully receive God's gift of salvation. To enable us to make that faithful response, we are now illumined and empowered by the Holy Spirit to glorify God and so "walk in the newness of life" that we will be related to our neighbors with "just loving and loving justice."

## The Role of the Church

For the nurture of believers and the carrying out of the ministry of reconciliation, the triune God calls the church into existence and makes it faithful and visible for the world. In the fellowship of the Spirit, the Lordship of Christ is confessed, God is worshiped, the sacraments are administered, and the coming kingdom is anticipated and prayed for. Ultimately, these events lead to God's redemption of all things. Between now and then, believers are called to be faithful in glorifying and enjoying God, in caring for God's new creation, in loving God's new beings, in making peace with justice a reality everywhere, and in witnessing through word and deed to God's gracious gift of salvation. It is in this context that pastoral care offered to Smith is located. Through suffering love and liberating power God will bring the kingdom into being for those who will receive it. And believers are assured of God's faithfulness even as they pray: "Thy kingdom come, Thy will be done . . . give us . . . forgive us . . . lead us not . . . but deliver us . . . for thine is the Kingdom, the Power, and the Glory, forever."

Redeemed people of God, those who have been grasped by grace and given faith to hope and love, are to manifest God's wholeness, salvation, and healing that they have been given in God's new creation. The triune God intends "life abundantly" (*perisos zoe*), or "life in all its fullness," and "life eternal" (*aionios zoe*), or "life in its highest quality," resulting in wholeness, soundness, and righteousness which constitutes true health and holiness. In a benediction St. Paul prayed: "May God, the God of peace, make you holy in every part, and keep you sound in spirit, soul, and body, without fault when our Lord Jesus Christ comes."[27]

Salvation is the gift of God, and wholeness is the promise of God. In the face of sin, sickness, oppression, suffering, even death itself, the redeemed community is grounded in the stubborn hope that nothing can finally thwart the creative, redemptive, life-renewing purpose of God for humankind.

I have given much of my life to a ministry of pastoral care and counseling. I know, however, that those expressions of ministry are but little fingers on the arm of the church's total ministry. Further, this essay presents but a limited piece of either the human predicament or the revelation of God. In fact, in the time you have taken to read this essay, massive human needs and untold human ills have gone unattended. By mid-afternoon on any day, ten thousand children will have starved to death, four thousand will have been brutally beaten by their parents, and one thousand will have been raped. Unjust systems and unrighteous persons in places of authority will have added to the hellish existence of many people on this planet earth.

In a village of a hundred people that is a microcosm of the globe, seventy are unable to read, more than fifty are suffering from malnutrition, and more than eighty live in substandard housing. Six of those villagers are Americans, but they consume 80 percent of the village's total energy and receive one third of the village's total income. That is how life in God's world is being experienced by the masses.

Before this day ends, God's healing will have been reduced to what some medical doctor or some pastoral counselor can do to relieve a pain or some anguish. Or the general welfare will be reduced to some instrument of destruction in the name of national defense in order to make some Podunk Hollow "safe for democracy." Or deliverance will be relegated to some part of the ocean or the desert where we will store nuclear waste that will cause some other generation to die.

Or wholeness will be reduced to some sumptuous consumerism, some stock piling of goods so that life in this world will be more comfortable for me and mine. And all the while, the wholeness and salvation intended by the God of the universe continues to tremble with inexpressible mystery, a mystery that humanity can never seem to grasp but a mystery that nevertheless continues to address us in the totality of our essence and our existence.

In the meantime, even the healthiest, the most holy, those knowing the zenith of wholeness, must surely know that even they have only a foretaste of what already is but is not yet, neither personally nor corporately. And they, like the wandering Israelite, still long for that which only God, the Healer, can give.

# Notes

## Introduction

1. Victor Paul Furnish, in *A Biblical Basis for Ministry*, ed. Earl E. Shelp and Ronald Sunderland (Philadelphia: Westminster Press, 1978), p. 102.
2. Ibid., p. 135.
3. D. Moody Smith, in *A Biblical Basis for Ministry*, p. 226.
4. See Ronald H. Sunderland, "Lay Pastoral Care," *Journal of Pastoral Care* 52, no. 2 (Summer 1988): 159–171.
5. See, e.g., Herbert Anderson, "The Congregation: Health Center or Healing Community," *Word and World* 9, no. 2 (Spring 1989): 123–131; also Liston O. Mills in this volume.
6. For further reading in this area, see William B. Oglesby Jr., *Biblical Themes for Pastoral Care* (Nashville: Abingdon Press, 1980); John Patton, *Is Human Forgiveness Possible?* (Nashville: Abingdon Press, 1985).

## Chapter 1

1. The wisdom literature of scripture referred to includes the wisdom Psalms, Proverbs, Ecclesiastes, and Job. In addition, when referring to wisdom tradition, scholars normally include the later apocryphal writings: Ecclesiasticus and the Wisdom of Solomon.
2. *New Yorker*, 19 December 1988.
3. Diane Bergund, SA, *What They Are Saying About Wisdom Literature* (New York: Paulist Press, 1984), p. 4.
4. Zoe White, *The Art of the Every Day* (Wallingford, Pa.: Pendle Hill Pamphlet 281, 1988), p. 9.
5. Peter Taylor, "The Promise of Rain," in *The Old Friend and Other Stories* (New York: Ballantine Books, 1985), p. 109.

6. Alastair V. Campbell, *Professionalism and Pastoral Care* (Philadelphia: Fortress Press, 1985), p. 40.
7. Edwin H. Friedman, *Generation to Generation: Family Process in Church and Society* (New York: Guilford Press, 1988), pp. 207–209.
8. Don S. Browning, *Religious Ethics and Pastoral Care* (Philadelphia: Fortress Press, 1983), p. 16.
9. Thomas Merton, *Conjectures of a Guilty Bystander* (New York: Doubleday, 1965), p. 65.

## Chapter 2

1. G. Ernest Wright, *The Old Testament Against Its Environment* (London: SCM Press, 1950), pp. 44–45.
2. See Daniel Levenson, *Seasons of a Man's Life* (New York: Alfred A. Knopf, 1978), p. 335; Carol Gilligan, *In a Different Voice* (Cambridge, Mass.: Harvard University Press, 1982); Jack Balswick, *The Inexpressive Male* (Lexington, Mass.: Lexington Books, 1988).
3. For a discussion of the psychological issues of co-dependence, see the books of Anne Wilson Schaef, especially *Co-Dependence: Misunderstood-Mistreated* (San Francisco: Harper and Row, 1986).

## Chapter 3

1. For a good summary of this movement, see Don S. Browning, *Religious Thought and the Modern Psychologies* (Philadelphia: Fortress Press, 1987), pp. 61–93; also, Browning, "The Pastoral Counselor as Ethicist: What Difference Do We Make," *The Journal of Pastoral Care* 42, no. 4 (Winter 1988): 294.
2. See Don S. Browning, *The Moral Context of Pastoral Care* (Philadelphia: Westminster Press, 1976).
3. Smith, Edward W. L., *The Body in Psychotherapy* (Jefferson, N.C.: McFarland and Co., 1985), p. 3.
4. Quoted in ibid.
5. Boston Women's Health Collective, *Our Bodies, Ourselves* (New York: Simon and Schuster, 1979), p. 3.
6. I have used some of the illustrative material that follows in a

different and more expanded form in *The Intimate Connection: Male Sexuality, Masculine Spirituality* (Philadelphia: Westminster Press, 1988).

7. Martin Buber, *I and Thou*, trans. by Walter Kaufman (New York: Charles Scribner and Sons, 1970), p. 69. Carter Heyward's work puts Buber's relational theology into a radically incarnational Christian interpretation. See especially her *Redemption of God* (Washington, D.C.: University Press of America, 1982) and "In the Beginning is the Relation: Toward a Christian Ethic of Sexuality," *Integrity Forum* 7, no. 2 (Lent 1981).

8. Cf. Beverly Wildung Harrison, "Human Sexuality and Mutuality," in Judith L. Weidman, ed., *Christian Feminism* (New York: Harper and Row, 1984), especially pp. 147ff.

9. Pierre Teilhard de Chardin, *Science and Christ* (New York: Harper and Row, 1968), pp. 12f.

### Chapter 4

1. John McNeill, *History of the Cure of Souls* (New York: Harper, 1951), p. vii.

2. Seward Hiltner, *Preface to Pastoral Theology* (New York: Abingdon, 1958); W. Clebsch and C. Jaeckle, *Pastoral Care in Historical Perspective* (Englewood Cliffs, N.J.: Prentice-Hall, 1964).

3. Theodore Tappert, *Luther's Letters of Spiritual Counsel* (London: SCM Press, 1955), p. 15.

4. H. Richard Niebuhr and D. Williams, eds., *The Ministry in Historical Perspective* (New York: Harper and Row, 1956), pp. 193–206.

5. Ibid.

6. Philip Rieff, *The Triumph of the Therapeutic* (New York: Harper and Row, 1966), p. 7.

7. Don Browning, *Religious Ethics and Pastoral Care* (Philadelphia: Fortress Press, 1983), pp. 32–36.

8. See Don Browning, *Practical Theology* (New York: Harper and Row, 1983), pp. 21–41.

9. Robert Bellah et al., *Habits of the Heart: Individualism and Commitment in American Life* (Berkeley: University of California Press, 1985).

10. Ernest Becker, *The Denial of Death* (New York: Macmillan, 1973), p. 52.

## Chapter 5

1. Roy Schaffer, *The Analytic Attitudes* (New York: Basic Books, 1983); Gerald Egan, *The Skilled Helper: A Model for Systematic Helping and Interpersonal Relating* (Monterey, Ca.: Brooks/ Cole, 1975).
2. M. L. Smith, G. V. Glass, and T. J. Miller, *The Benefits of Psychotherapy* (Baltimore: Johns Hopkins Press, 1980).
3. Edgar H. Schein, "Personal Change Through Interpersonal Relationships," in Warren Bennis et al., eds., *Essays in Interpersonal Dynamics* (Homewood, Ill.: Dorsey Press, 1979), pp. 129–162.
4. Carl R. Rogers, *On Becoming a Person* (Boston: Houghton Mifflin, 1970); William Damon and Daniel Hart, *Self-Understanding in Childhood and Adolescence* (Cambridge: Cambridge University Press, 1988).
5. Daniel Stern, *The Interpersonal World of the Infant* (New York: Basic Books, 1984); Paul Ekman, "Expressions and the Nature of Emotion," in Klaus R. Scherer and Paul Ekman, eds., *Approaches to Emotion* (Hillsdale, N.J.: Lawrence Erlbaum, 1984).
6. Paul Ekman, *Telling Lies* (New York: Berkeley Books, 1985).
7. Jerome D. Frank, *Persuasion and Healing: A Comparative Study of Psychotherapy* (Baltimore: Johns Hopkins Press, 1973); Lawrence M. Brammer, *The Helping Relationship: Process and Skills* (Englewood Cliffs, N.J.: Prentice-Hall, 1973), ch. 2.
8. Albert Ellis and Russell Grieger, *Handbook of Rational-Emotive Therapy* (New York: Springer Publishing Co., 1977); Aaron T. Beck, *Cognitive Therapy and the Emotional Disorders* (New York: International Universities Press, 1976).
9. Stephen Toulmin, "The Tyranny of Principles: Regaining the Ethics of Discretion," *The Hastings Center Report* (December 1981), pp. 31–39.
10. Morris B. Parloff, Irene Elkin Waskow, and Barry E. Wolfe, "Research on Therapist Variables in Relation to Process and Outcome," in Sol L. Garfield and Allen E. Bergin, eds.,

*Handbook of Psychotherapy and Behavior Change: An Empirical Analysis*, 2nd. ed. (New York: John Wiley and Sons, 1978), pp. 233–282.

11. Dianna E. Hartley and Hans H. Stroup, "The Therapeutic Alliance: Its Relationship to Outcome in Brief Psychotherapy," in Joseph Masling, ed., *Empirical Studies of Psychoanalytical Theories* (Hillsdale, N.J.: Analytic Press, 1983), pp. 1–37.

12. Mary Midgley, "The Flight from Blame," *Philosophy* 12 (1987): 123–134; Sidney Callahan, "The Role of Emotion in Ethical Decision Making," *The Hastings Center Report* (June/July 1988), pp. 9–14.

13. Daniel Goleman, *Vital Lies, Simple Truths: The Psychology of Self-Deception* (New York: Simon and Schuster, 1985); Iris Murdoch, *The Sovereignty of Good* (London: Ark Paperbacks, 1985), pp. 35–45.

14. Sidney Callahan, *With All Our Heart and Mind: The Spiritual Works of Mercy in a Psychological Age* (New York: Crossroad, 1988), pp. 21–37; John C. Hoffman, *Ethical Confrontation in Counseling* (Chicago: University of Chicago Press, 1979).

15. Henri Nouwen, *The Wounded Healer* (New York: Doubleday, 1972).

## Chapter 6

1. Shirley C. Guthrie Jr., *Christian Doctrine: Teachings of the Christian Church* (Richmond, Va.; CLC Press, 1968), p. 27.

2. Descartes's dualistic theory postulated a real world of matter that was subject to natural law and an equally real world of thought in a mind that was free. All matter could be reduced to local motion and could be understood and controlled by reason and logic. Newton provided laws of motion that reduced the focus of nature to mathematical terms, and the world of matter was now composed of inert substances, governed by mathematical laws. Bacon added that nature could be understood only through systematic experimentation, but once nature was reduced to understandable parts, it could be controlled.

3. Jurgen Moltmann, *The Power of the Powerless* (London: SCM Press, 1983), p. 142.

4. Quoted in Frank Wright, *The Pastoral Nature of Healing* (London: SCM Press, 1985), p. 12.

5. In most instances today, a publicly sanctioned pastoral counselor is specially trained, ecclesiastically credentialed, professionally certified, and licensed by the state. Standards for certification as a pastoral counselor may be obtained from the American Association of Pastoral Counselors, 9508A Lee Highway, Fairfax, Va. 22031.

6. William B. Oglesby Jr., *Biblical Themes for Pastoral Care* (Nashville: Abingdon Press, 1980), p. 42. By "atypical" Oglesby meant "the scheduling of regular weekly sessions consisting of purposefully limited duration, i.e., fifty-five minutes, to continue over an indefinite series of sessions until the parishioner(s) can function without such an arrangement [p. 229]."

7. In his book *Protestant Pastoral Counseling* (Philadelphia: Westminster Press, 1962), Oates described the uniqueness of pastoral counseling as a "spiritual conversation" that involves a meeting of two persons in the context of the Christian faith and a dialogue between them concerning (1) "their way of life in times past," (2) "the decisive turnings of the living present," and (3) "the consideration of the outcome of their life [p. 168]." In this conceptualization of pastoral counseling, Oates called for a real presence from both, a dialogical conversation between both, and an active participation with the parishioner in three dimensions of time within the context and utilizing the content of the Christian faith.

8. Wayne E. Oates, *Pastoral Counseling* (Philadelphia: Westminster Press, 1974), pp. 11–13.

9. Edward E. Thornton, *Theology and Pastoral Counseling* (Philadelphia: Fortress Press, 1964), pp. 27–37. Thornton was taking a stance over against Eduard Thurneysen and others who assume the task of pastoral counseling to be that of proclaiming the content of scripture (both its message about grace and its ethical demands). He contends that the "way-preparer" can speak only penultimate words, never ultimate ones (cf. pp. 38–55). The ultimate word is spoken by the triune God: it is the word that both client and counselor are justified and sanctified by grace through faith. How one prepares the way for the

hearing and receiving of that ultimate word comprises the art and skill of pastoral counseling.

10. See Seward Hiltner, *Preface to Pastoral Theology: The Ministry and Theory of Shepherding* (New York: Abingdon Press, 1958). Note especially Hiltner's footnotes on pp. 216–224.

11. See Thomas Oden, *Kerygma and Counseling* (Philadelphia: Westminster Press, 1966), in which Oden tried to relate the psychotherapy of Carl Rogers with Barthian theology. He moves from God to humanity through an analogy of faith and claims that there is an implicit assumption hidden in effective psychotherapy that is made explicit in the Christian proclamation. In his *Contemporary Theology and Psychotherapy* (Philadelphia: Westminster Press, 1967), Oden seeks to clarify how the theology of Dietrich Bonhoeffer, Pierre Teilhard de Chardin, and Paul Tillich have potential relevance for the emergent forms of psychotherapy. In his more recent publications, Oden has focused on the broader ministry of pastoral care with the intent of relating that ministry to the classical disciplines of theology and more explicitly to the early church fathers.

12. Wayne E. Oates, *Pastoral Counseling* (Philadelphia: Westminster Press, 1974), pp. 13f, 20–23. Oates asserts that "pastoral counseling is concerned with the growth of a mature conscience," that "the prophetic concern for doing justly, loving mercy, and walking humbly with God is the 'stance of being' and the 'angle of vision' that makes counseling pastoral [p. 13]," and that "pastoral counseling is sweaty participation with persons in their life and death struggle for moral integrity in relation to God [p. 14]."

13. The primary resource for this perspective is in Browning's *The Moral Context of Pastoral Counseling* (Philadelphia: Westminster Press, 1976). In a book edited by Browning, *Practical Theology: The Emerging Field in Theology, Church, and World* (San Francisco: Harper and Row, Publishers, 1983), he acknowledges that in *The Moral Context of Pastoral Counseling*, he "defined pastoral theology as the theology of pastoral acts of care and associated practical theology with the task of developing a moral theology of the human life cycle. I am now willing to define pastoral theology as dealing with both (a) a moral theology of the human life cycle and (b) a theology of pastoral

acts of care. Practical theology I now associate with the larger task of writing theology from the perspective of action in contrast to belief, the latter being the major task of systematic theology. In this perspective theological ethics is a division of practical theology [p. 201]."

14. Hiltner, *Preface*, p. 24. This is Hiltner's term for "pastoral theology."

15. Smith stated that he was born soon after World War II, the eldest of three children and the only son.

His father had been something of a war hero, but he had abandoned his family when Smith was five. He died a drunk when Smith was thirteen, but Smith didn't have much contact with him after he left the family. Smith's mother never remarried and still lives near Smith. They attend the same church and usually have Sunday dinner together, and Smith tends to her place and manages her finances. The sisters are both married now and live in distant cities. The older one was a bit wild for a while, and the younger one was always somewhat sickly. Smith has no recollection of his paternal grandparents and no connection with any relative of his father. Both maternal grandparents are dead, but he has fond memories of "Grannie" Jones.

Smith was an Eagle Scout and a serious student. He played some sandlot sports but had to work after age sixteen. He worked his way through college and an evening MBA program at the state university. He had no really close friends in school and dated only once or twice. He met Betty when he was doing his MBA. She was working on a degree in accounting and did secretarial work near where Smith worked.

Betty's father had abandoned his family for another woman when Betty was thirteen. She didn't like or trust men, but she was attracted to Smith's seriousness and dependability. They didn't have much time or money to date often but they felt comfortable together.

They married when Smith was twenty-six and soon had two sons, who are now thirteen and fifteen. Betty has found her joy in being a doting mother, a supportive helpmate, and a faithful church worker. Smith is the sole wage earner of the family, but he has done well enough for them to have an old Chevy and a new Honda. They live in a ranch-style home in one of the better school districts.

Smith is at present a supervisor of a dozen or so people with a multi-national corporation. He experiences constant pressure about the bottom-line profit margin, but his real hassle is having to deal with lazy, unmotivated employees whom he cannot terminate. He's impatient with their slowness and ineptness. Rather than delegate work to them, he just does it himself. Smith has no close friends at work and cannot trust his director. In fact, he knows his newest director does not appreciate his work or value his person.

Smith's only hobby is collecting toy railroad box cars and constructing an electric train track. He has no other particular form of recreation. His weekends are spent working in his or his mother's yard or doing odd jobs of repair. He can't get his lazy sons to help him because they're always playing ball or something. He and Betty rarely go out, seldom are invited anywhere, and never have anyone over. He's just not much into chit-chat or gossip. He did serve as an elder once, but that was for the birds—too much politics going on in that bunch for him.

16. See Daniel Day Williams, *The Minister and the Care of Souls* (New York: Harper and Brothers, Publishers, 1961), p. 17. "To love means to conform our actions to the concrete needs of the neighbor. . . . To know, therefore, that we are to love our neighbor does not tell us what we are to do, until we discover our neighbor's needs and learn what we can do." Carroll A. Wise defined pastoral caring as "the art of communicating the inner meaning of the gospel (God's accepting of persons revealed in Christ and transmitted through loving relationships) to persons at the point of their need." cf. Wise, *The Meaning of Pastoral Care* (New York: Harper and Row, Publishers, 1966), p. 8.

17. See Romans 12:5; 1 Corinthians 12:12–27; Ephesians 4:25.

18. Paul Tillich, *Systematic Theology*, vol. 2 (Chicago: University of Chicago Press, 1957), pp. 231–237. In his discussion of sanctification, Tillich uses these categories as "four principles determining the New Being as process."

19. Carroll A. Wise, *Pastoral Psychotherapy: Theory and Practice* (New York: Jason Aronson, 1980), p. xii.

20. John Patton, *Pastoral Counseling: A Ministry of the Church* (Nashville: Abingdon Press, 1983), p. 212.

21. Ibid., p. 220.

22. See Hiltner, *Preface*, p. 89. "Healing means becoming whole . . . , actually a rebecoming, a restoration of a condition once obtaining but then lost. . . . Thus, healing is to be understood as the process of restoring functional wholeness." Also, Clebsch and Jaeckle define healing as "a pastoral function that aims to overcome some impairment by restoring a person to wholeness and by leading him to advance beyond his previous condition. . . . In the Christian pastoral understanding of healing, however, healing is more than mere restoration, for it includes a forward gain over the condition prevailing before illness [p. 33]." "Healing as restoration and advance has always been an important function of the ministry of the cure of souls [p. 34]." See William A. Clebsch and Charles Jaeckle, *Pastoral Care in Historical Perspective* (New York: Jason Aronson, 1975).

23. See Deuteronomy 26:5–10.

24. John Wilkinson, *Health and Healing: Studies in New Testament Principles and Practice* (Edinburgh: Handsel Press, 1980), p. 5.

25. See Leviticus 19:2 (TEV).

26. See Ephesians 2:10, 15, 4:24; Romans 6:4, 7:6; Galatians 6:15; 2 Corinthians 5:17; Colossians 3:10.

27. See 1 Thessalonians 5:23 (NEB).